D0011492

the

SPIRITUAL POWER

of
empathy

About the Author

Cyndi Dale (Minneapolis, MN) is an internationally renowned author, speaker, healer, and business consultant. She is president of Life Systems Services, through which she has conducted over 35,000 client sessions and presented training classes throughout Europe, Asia, and the Americas. Visit her online at CyndiDale.com.

CYNDI DALE

the

SPIRITUAL
POWER

of
empathy

Develop Your Intuitive Gifts
for Compassionate Connection

Llewellyn Publications
WOODBURY, MINNESOTA

The Spiritual Power of Empathy: Develop Your Intuitive Gifts for Compassionate Connection © 2014 by Cyndi Dale. All rights reserved. No part of this book may be used or reproduced in any manner whatsoever, including Internet usage, without written permission from Llewellyn Publications, except in the case of brief quotations embodied in critical articles and reviews.

FIRST EDITION
Fourth Printing, 2015

Book design by Rebecca Zins
Cover design by Ellen Lawson
Cover and interior floral pattern: iStockphoto.com/30520330/©Suriko
Chakra figure base art by Wendy Froshay; additional
modifications by Llewellyn Art Department

Llewellyn Publications is a registered trademark of Llewellyn Worldwide Ltd.

Library of Congress Cataloging-in-Publication Data
Dale, Cyndi.
 The spiritual power of empathy: develop your intuitive gifts for compassionate
connection / Cyndi Dale.
      pages   cm
 Includes bibliographical references.
 ISBN 978-0-7387-3799-7
 1. Parapsychology. 2. Extrasensory perception. 3. Empathy. 4. Intuition.
 5. Compassion. I. Title.
 BF1040.D35 2014
 133.8—dc23
                                                                              2014020480

Llewellyn Worldwide Ltd. does not participate in, endorse, or have any authority or responsibility concerning private business transactions between our authors and the public.
   All mail addressed to the author is forwarded, but the publisher cannot, unless specifically instructed by the author, give out an address or phone number.
   Any Internet references contained in this work are current at publication time, but the publisher cannot guarantee that a specific location will continue to be maintained. Please refer to the publisher's website for links to authors' websites and other sources.

Llewellyn Publications
A Division of Llewellyn Worldwide Ltd.
2143 Wooddale Drive
Woodbury, MN 55125-2989
www.llewellyn.com

Printed in the United States of America

contents

PART II: APPLICATION
Mastering the Gift of Empathy

EMPATHIC EXPLORATIONS

Introduction

If pressed to define or describe empathy, most of us might describe it in a one-dimensional way as a seemingly straightforward matter of imagining what another person might be going through, typically imagining what they are *feeling*. But after decades of work as an intuitive counselor and years of researching and writing about subtle-energy medicine and the applications of our intuitive and spiritual gifts, I have discovered that when it comes to empathy, we have been laboring under a misapprehension.

Before setting our misconceptions straight, though, it's important to point out that empathy has been the subject of inquiry and contemplation by a wide range of brilliant people, from psychologists and neurological experts to sages, saints, and healers. One of the contemporary authors and teachers who has contributed greatly to our understanding of empathy is Daniel Goleman, PhD, whose work I will discuss briefly in part I. By differentiating between cognitive empathy, emotional empathy, and what he refers to as empathic concern, Goleman has opened new doors of awareness into these innate capacities.

Still, despite the important insights that he and many thinkers have offered toward our understanding of empathy, too often it is seen as *one* capacity rather than a *collection* of gifts. Through my work I have come to know that empathy goes far beyond the fairly simplistic understanding most of us have of it. Empathy encompasses thoughts, perceptions, sensations, and almost every other sort of awareness we are blessed with—including psychic gifts—and it extends not only to other individuals but also to groups, animals, plants, and even objects in nature. In my view, when our empathic abilities are fully developed, they involve a multidimensional set of spiritual abilities operating powerfully at the level of the subtle body, which is a set of structures that run on subtle, or hard to recognize, energy. Our subtle energy anatomy is composed of energy channels (such as the meridians), energy bodies (including the chakras), and energy fields (such as the auric field). And when that power is engaged, we become capable of profound levels of connection and understanding.

Empathy is bandied about as if we know what it is, but it is really so much more than what can be defined in a dictionary entry or even in an entire psychology textbook; it includes but also transcends psychology. Of course, at the deepest level, we already *do* know the beauty of empathy—beyond any and all descriptions—and this book will reacquaint you with your inborn empathic capacity in ways that just might transform the way you see and how you live.

Empathy and Our Psychic Gifts

The key to unleashing the power of empathy is to understand all the levels of empathy that are potentially available to you, including those considered psychic or esoteric. Many esoteric professionals use the term *clairempathy*, meaning "clear feeling," referring to a stand-alone psychic skill that allows you to experience the thoughts, emotions, and symptoms of others. But the way I see and experience it, empathy is more multidimensional than the term implies; empathy involves a whole *set* of subtle-energy or psychic abilities, as well as more commonly recognized skills such as the ability to simply be present and listen. So I choose not to use the word clairempathy. For me, empathy as an umbrella term is more meaningful because it encompasses the full spectrum of the empathic experience, both subtle and worldly. As with other words that have great meaning to us, such as *love* or *caring*, it represents many levels of a rich, heartfelt experience. In the case of empathy, the experience is one of *connection*.

We all love to connect. More importantly, we *need* to connect. Infants lacking bonding often fail to thrive; the elderly locked into their isolated apartments become lonely and depressed. There are behaviors and attitudes that can enable connection and care or inhibit and prevent the same. A subtle or inaudible thought about someone can create a pathway of compassion if it is caring, for it will be felt by the other. But hold a judgment in your mind, such as "that person looks weird," and immediately they will register this subtle attitude and shut down. The sum of all ways we increase connectivity through these often silent exchanges could be called empathy.

The Three Mechanisms of Psychic Empathy

The subtle-energy gifts involved in empathy can be thought of as the mechanisms that allow us to be empathic. They can work independently, in small combinations, or all at once.

I refer to the first set of mechanisms as the bodily empathic gifts because they are ways in which empathy registers in our own bodies as a direct physical experience. They include:

- clear sensing (clairsentience), which can manifest emotionally or mentally
- clear tasting (clairgustance)
- clear smelling (clairscent)
- clear touching (clairtangency)
- clear knowing (claircognizance)

In addition, two other sets of subtle abilities—and these are psychic gifts you may be more familiar with—can come into play in the empathic experience:

- clear seeing (clairvoyance), the ability to psychically see information
- clear hearing (clairaudience), the ability to psychically hear information

Unlike the first set of empathic gifts, which register in the body as physical sensation, clairvoyance and clairaudience offer insights and information that register in the mind (the "mind's eye" or the "mind's ear"). I consider them to be sets of abilities as well because each can take multiple forms. For instance, a clairvoyant person might psychically receive a message about someone else's experience through an image, a symbol, a color, or even a moving slide show. A clairaudient person might intuitively hear words, sentences, music, or tones.

Together, these three sets of abilities—the bodily empathic gifts, clairvoyance, and clairaudience—compose the three main spiritual gifts that support the development of your spiritual nature.

We will more fully explore the empathic clairs in upcoming chapters, but there is even more to your empathic gifts than these! As you will learn in chapter 2, every spiritual center in your body is associated with one or more psychic gifts; most of these are bodily empathic. Only two are devoted entirely to the spiritual gifts of clairvoyance and clairaudience. By examining all the psychic abilities in this context, you will discover all the ways in which your entire energetic body is primed for empathic connection.

Overall, empathy is a vital pathway for continually transforming our physical experiences into spiritual lessons. It also leads us directly to the door of compassion, that inner call to ease another's pain by putting our empathy into action—an essential and timely topic that we will fully explore in the pages of this book.

Six Empathic Styles

Your empathy experience may include any or all of the clairs I have just listed, depending on your natural gifts and inclinations. In addition to identifying these abilities, through my work with clients, my research, and personal experience, I have found that there are six distinct *styles* of empathy: physical, emotional, mental, natural, spiritual, and shamanic.

Please note: I use the term *shamanic* to recognize the ancient and cross-cultural meaning of the word. Since the late twentieth century, many esoterics have affiliated shamanism with only plant medicine, or the invocation of a trance style through the use of substances such as hallucinogens. Though some shamans in some cultures have used this means to promote a spiritual or healing state, my studies and experience would greatly downplay this fact. Shamans employ a vast toolkit of activities to promote health, including herbs, chanting, dancing, art, and mediumship. They are truly holistic practitioners of the spiritual and natural arts.

You'll learn about these six empathic styles in depth throughout the book, learn to recognize them in yourself and others, and acquire valuable tools to help you make the most of your empathic abilities, no matter what your style may be.

I cannot emphasize enough that the six types all have a common purpose: they provide connection. Connection is the key to not only understanding empathy, but also to having its extraordinary powers infuse our daily lives. Empathy is the great connector. It is the bridge that brings us close again—close to ourselves, to others, and to the Divine in all its formed and formless glory. No matter how much personal hurt or collective pain has separated us before, empathy can bring us together again.

In essence, I believe that empathy is the single most important vehicle we have for accessing love on this planet. It is coded into us physically, and we connect with it emotionally. Our use of it is controlled by our belief systems and mental capacities. Essentially, however, it allows us to mirror the Greater Spirit. Understanding the six empathic styles helps us to expand beyond the person-to-person connection, as important as that is. It is through our personal use of these gifts that we find connection with all that is.

Your Own Journey as an Empath

Each of us is part of a much larger sphere of consciousness, and deepening your capacity to connect with that larger sphere is the purpose of this book. As you are an integral and precious part of the larger sphere, I have written this book for *you*, exactly where you are now in your empathic journey.

Since you have already begun your voyage through these pages, it's very likely that you can relate to one or more of the following categories of readers:

1) You know you are empathic and are often overwhelmed by incoming sensations and information.
2) You feel that your heightened sensitivity to people, places, or energies is cause for trouble in your life.
3) You believe that empaths are other people, not you. But still, you find yourself drawn to discover more.
4) You want to make more loving, safe connections with others. You feel a great deal of compassion for people, animals, and perhaps nature itself, and you want to know how to put that compassion into action.

There was a time when I found myself in category 1 (and teetering into category 2) most of the time, constantly swallowed up by sensations I couldn't understand or regulate. Bombarded by all the incoming and upwelling data, I would sometimes shut down and find myself unable to connect and bond at all. I just wasn't at ease with taking on the intensity of energy and feelings that continually washed over me. And I was afraid that I would have to take care of everyone I was connecting with, that I would be enmeshed in a kind of energetic codependency.

It probably won't surprise you to know that I was sometimes enmeshed anyway. How could it be otherwise? Being resistant to my empathic nature, I was sure to experience what I was pushing so hard against.

But that was in my early days, before I discovered that empathy is one of my greatest allies; in fact, I would say that empathy is the beating heart of my life as a teacher, mother, and lover of humanity.

How This Book Is Organized

While I have written this book to convey my and others' discoveries about empathy in all its forms—findings that are both broad and deep in nature—I also wrote it as a practical guide to expanded awareness of empathy and how it operates for you. As you read stories from my own life and those of my clients, you can expect to have your own aha moments, perhaps seeing yourself reflected in the experiences that I share in the chapters ahead. You might have a kind of reunion with your inner self, connecting dots that you haven't thought about in a very long time. And through the steps, tools, techniques, and tips offered herein, you will soon be prepared to call on your empathic powers anytime you want or need them.

Part I builds a foundation of understanding of what empathy is and the myriad ways it is experienced—essential information that will give you an important context for the discussions and practices in part II. Chapter 1 offers an orientation to key concepts, and here you will have the opportunity to work with your first "empathic exploration"—a series of exercises I have sprinkled throughout the chapters of part I to help you reflect upon and explore how empathy works in your own life, even before you get into the practical applications contained in part II.

In chapter 2 you will learn that empathy and the body are linked by an unbreakable bond—that you are physically wired to connect. Then, as you enter chapter 3, you will dive headlong into the pool of compassion, coming to understand compassion as the true catalyst for turning empathy into meaningful action.

With that, the stage will be set for you to discover your empathic style in chapter 4, where you will learn in detail about the six empathic types in order to identify where your strongest inclinations lie.

In part II you will learn how this all applies to your life—how to work with the strengths of your own empathic style in real-world situations. Here you will gain access to the three primary tools that make up the empath's medicine bag, including the most important techniques and practices I use every day in my counseling sessions and as I go about the business of my life. These are the techniques I use to remain connected to the Divine and guided by my inner wisdom. One of these is the five steps to compassionate empathy, which forms the map to healing yourself and others with your empathic gifts. Discovering ways to appropriately apply the five steps to relationships, work, parenting, and life will leave you well equipped to put your finely honed empathic skills into action right away.

Finally, for those who are eager to deepen their knowledge and widen their perspective on empathy, I have included two detailed appendices, the first examining the critical distinction between sympathy and empathy, and the second exploring the "impaired empath": those who are either too empathic to function well or are shut down and cut off from their empathic abilities. In these appendices I cover issues I am frequently asked about in my practice. People often seek my help with these real-life dilemmas, which we all encounter as part of the human family. So once you have established a foundation of knowledge in part I and learned the practical techniques of part II, I invite you to take the time to explore these discussions of common empathy-related experiences.

Empathy: The Poetry of the Soul

Like every other person I have met, you have probably been bruised once or twice in matters of love. We have all experienced everything from a mild hesitation about connecting with another to a deep fear of loving and being loved. Stemming from moments of shame, rejection, and loss, and weighed down by some measure of doubt as to our worthiness as human beings, many of us find ourselves afraid to love at times—afraid to connect with a world that needs us.

I understand the "wait and see" attitude around love. But I can't sit back and let this be the way of things because while some of us are driving down the highway of love with the brakes on, chances to connect are passing us by! And I'm not speaking only of romantic love; I mean love in all its idiosyncratic splendor, whether it's the love of a dear friend, a cousin, a son or daughter, a cherished pet, or anyone else.

Therefore, my hope is that through this book you can know that *love and connection are safe*. In fact, I'm going to show you how to know that they are safe and how to make them safe—two sides of the same coin. I hope you will take that coin and spend it generously.

You see, the poetry of our soul *is* compassionate connection. As you are about to discover, the empathic gifts encourage qualities of connection and bonding that allow us to soar to new heights of love. In this way they promote our ultimate spiritual purpose, which is to learn about love. They do this by inviting us to move beyond our individual selves and experience the joy that comes from greater closeness and intimacy with all of life.

PART I

Foundation

Discovering the Gift of Empathy

The excitement of discovery is about to begin! In addition to uncovering new dimensions of empathy, including its profound relationship to compassion and how empathy differs from sympathy, you will learn about the energetic pathways it takes through the physical, emotional, and spiritual layers of your being. You will come to understand that you are literally wired to connect, sense, know, and feel in sync with your highest wisdom. And as you begin to understand your own empathic style more fully in the chapters ahead, your soul will be delighted that you are reclaiming the extraordinary spiritual power known as empathy.

CHAPTER 1

Your Empathic Gifts: The Clairs

The friend who can be silent with us in a moment of despair or confusion, who can stay with us in an hour of grief and bereavement, who can tolerate not knowing, not curing, not healing and face with us the reality of our powerlessness, that is a friend who cares.

HENRI J. M. NOUWEN, THE ROAD TO DAYBREAK

When he was just five years old, my youngest son crept into bed with me late one evening.

"Hey, Gabe," I whispered, making room for him, knowing this would be a tumultuous sleep full of little kid kicks and mutterings. "Couldn't you sleep?"

"No, Mommy," he said. "You are upset. I thought I could make it better."

How would a five-year-old know what his mom in the other room is experiencing? Along the same lines, how does anyone—like you, for instance—know what others sense, feel, or need without tangible proof?

We might ask other related questions about our ability to sense, feel, or know what is really going on outside ourselves in ways that seem uncanny or unusual. See if you can answer some of these in the affirmative:

- Have you ever had the experience of knowing what someone else is going through, even from a distance? Or knowing that someone is struggling even though they don't look upset and haven't expressed a concern?
- Have you ever tossed and turned all night because you just knew something was going to go wrong the next day, and then it did go really wrong?
- Do you sometimes sense another's bodily aches, pains, or illnesses as if they were your own?
- What about those disastrous get-togethers? You know the ones. You start the day in a perfectly good mood, and then you talk with a friend who's going through a hardship. By the time the conversation is over, you are so depressed, you're sagging—and your friend is fine.

You might also wonder about some other strange experiences you've had (none of which you would eagerly share with your doctor or therapist):

ROOM RAGE: You've only to enter a room (old houses are the worst) to sense what might have previously occurred there, from heated arguments to physical violence. (And it doesn't help that you can sometimes sense the former—and deceased—inhabitants.)

WEATHER "WOO WOO": Your body picks up on nature's stirrings before Doppler radar does. Way before a storm hits, you feel like you're plugged into a wall socket.

PLANETARY IMPROPRIETIES: Who needs to read an astronomy or astrology column? When Mercury is going retrograde, you are already experiencing the communication snafus that correlate to the shifts of this special planet.

LUCY LUNACY: You are the Lucy character in the *Peanuts* comic strip, and everyone is lining up, ready to pour their hearts out to you; the doctor is in. The problem is that you don't even make the five cents Lucy gets for the advice you dispense. In fact, all you ever get is drained and worn out.

HEALING HEART: Do you feel like you walk around with your hands at the ready, waiting to share healing with the world? Do you sometimes have to sit on your hands to keep yourself from helping everyone?

DOCTOR DOLITTLE: Remember Doctor Dolittle, the fictional character who could talk with the animals? You might not know how to formally speak animal—or plant, rock, or mineral—but you can sure sense what they are feeling.

HONESTY, SCHMONESTY: Your ability to sense whether others are being truthful rather than hypocritical is highly developed. It's like you have an internal honesty barometer—one that alerts you to other people's lapses of integrity.

EMPATHIC EXPLORATION 1   *Look to Your Own Experience*

These and many other sometimes mystifying experiences are all aspects of the wondrous, beautiful, and sometimes overwhelming abilities I described in the introduction, the psychic empathic gifts—the three sets of mechanisms at work in the subtle-body experience of empathy. Before we discuss those further, I invite you to take your first empathic exploration. The following questions will help you assess your own subtle-body experiences with empathy and how you feel about them.

- Can you recall a time when you entered a house and had a sense of what recently occurred there between inhabitants? Did you trust your perceptions?

- Have you ever held an object and perceived information about its owner? Were you able to prove the accuracy of your ideas?

- Do you frequently perceive a difference between how others act and what you feel they are truly experiencing emotionally? Which type of information—the way the other person appears or your feelings—has usually proven the most correct? Think about what this tells you about yourself and your giftedness.

- Can you remember an experience in which you switched emotions with someone? For instance, they started your time together feeling sad while you were happy, and by the time you were done with your exchange, *you* were sad and *they* were happy. What do you think this says about your empathic abilities?

- Is there someone in your life who seems to sap your energy? Describe how this happens for you and what you would like to be different in this relationship.

- Have you ever understood another's motives before they are able to do so themselves? Think about how you have used this information.

- How often do you sense what is occurring with animals or the other inhabitants of nature? Review what you usually do with this information—and what you might be able to do with it.

- How frequently do you sense the presence of invisible beings? Own your reaction to these beings; do they most frequently seem frightening or beneficent? Would you like more of these experiences, as long as they are positive?

The extraordinary sensory gifts and abilities you are using (whether consciously or not) when you have such experiences offer ways of knowing what is occurring in the environment around you, and not just with people but also with animals, other beings, objects, plants, planets, and even energies and entities across time. And the ways in which you use these gifts in your sensing of the world around you is a big factor in determining your empathic style. As I mentioned in the introduction, I have identified a total of six different empathic types or styles. You will learn about these in detail as you progress through the book, beginning in chapter 4.

Some of us employ only one or two of our subtle empathic abilities and some use more, but we are all empathically gifted. We are all "wired for sound," the sound being the songs and sensations of the universe. When you take the time to explore this invisible sensory world in your own life, what you learn can make all the difference in your empathic experiences from this point forward. You can choose to consciously develop all empathic styles or just your strongest ones. You can learn to rein them in or direct them toward what's best for you, engaging the world empathically in healthy ways.

Perhaps when you were growing up, people found your subtle abilities a little uncanny and deemed them "weird," so that's how you judge them yourself now. Maybe being empathic has never benefited you, only exhausted or controlled you. Or maybe your innate empathy, expressed through one or more of the styles you will soon learn about, is humming along just fine, and you want to deepen your understanding and exploration of it. No matter where you are with empathy, you can only benefit from enhancing this innate gift that invites compassionate bonding with the world around you.

What Is Empathy?

Empathy is typically defined as the capacity to share and understand others' emotions and needs as if they were our own. It also allows us to identify with others' ideas and experiences, as well as imagine what something or someone could become.

Yet empathy is so much more than this!

We often picture an empathetic person as someone who can walk in someone else's shoes. It's like you slip off your own moccasins—or boots, snowshoes, or sandals—and don another's. Because you can empathize, your capacity for caring about that other person, and perhaps even making a difference in his or her life, is greatly enhanced. This is why empathy is so often linked to compassion, or the ability to alleviate another's suffering.

Most of us have experienced empathic moments when we really feel what others are going through or understand what is occurring in their lives; maybe we've even followed a corresponding inner prompting to help. Because we can sense the private dilemmas of others, we may know exactly how to help them untie those knots. Empathy can stretch us in other directions, however, taking us beyond our comfort zone and into areas that aren't always considered "normal."

Some empathic people bond so completely with another person that they almost become that person in some ways, and this can go beyond the emotional and intellectual realms. They might take on someone else's physical injuries or childhood experiences. They might even tune in to potential future events, from catastrophes to job promotions to routine tasks. In fact, I had one client who was so empathic with her daughter that she moved heaven and earth to reach her by phone one day. When she did, she frantically blurted out, "Before you get that haircut, think again. You'll never be able to keep it up."

The daughter had been daydreaming about styling her hair in a 1960s beehive and had not discussed the plan with her mother. Meanwhile, her mother had been walking around for days imagining that her own hair was swept up in the archaic cone, obsessing about how challenging it would be to keep the shape smooth and under control. The mother had literally taken on her daughter's cosmetic fantasy, and when she finally figured out that she was empathizing with her daughter's idea and not her own, she rushed to "save the day"—or at least her daughter's hair.

As this example points out, there are many types of empathy. We can sense another's potential futures, thoughts, feelings, and needs, but sometimes the "other" isn't a person at all. Certain types of empaths have a wide relational range of motion. Sometimes they slide from sensing an aspect of another person to sensing the movement of a planet, the feelings of an animal, or the memories captured in an object.

I once worked with a young boy—I'll call him James—who could sense the energy in toys. He had only to pick up a toy that had been used by another child in order to assume that child's sense of reality.

This extreme sensory empathy enabled James to deeply understand other children's needs and lives. His serious brown eyes glowed as he discussed the time he had held a little girl's doll during first grade "show and tell" and knew that her mother was really sick. "Abby needed a hug," James explained. "So I gave her one, and that helped her a lot."

There were times, however, when James felt overloaded. "Sometimes I don't want to know something about other kids," he shared. "Especially if I don't like them."

As James discovered at such a young age, being empathic isn't without challenges. What we sense, we might become, perhaps to our own detriment, as was the case with one woman I worked with who was so empathic that she refused to leave her house.

"I can't help but know what everyone I meet is going through," she complained. "I once sat on the bus next to a homeless man, and I felt as if I'd been as mistreated by society as he had been."

Her empathic gifts were highly disturbing to her. Her discussion about her empathic sense of the homeless man concluded with this observation: "I got a dose of the misery of daily humiliation and ridicule. Not only did

I feel how sad he felt, but I also felt the presence of dark spirits around him telling him he didn't deserve any better."

The psychic empathic gifts can be as startlingly brilliant and insightful as they are overwhelmingly challenging and confusing. All in all, the subtle experience of empathy reminds me of a gripping poem by Walt Whitman called "There Was a Child Went Forth," which begins like this:

There was a child went forth every day,
And the first object he look'd upon, that object he became,
And that object became part of him for the day or a certain
part of the day, or for many years or stretching cycles of years…

Deep within each of us lies the ability to become what we are not: to hold this energy—the feeling, sense, and substance of it—for a day or for part of a day or perhaps for even longer. This is our empathic self.

During our time together through these pages, we will explore empathy from several angles, including empathy's physiological evidence as a biochemical ability and empathy's function as a social agreement, or a means to create safety within the tribe. First, however, it's important to embrace the subtle realms of empathy at their highest level, as the spiritual gifts that allow us to intuitively receive and interpret information from outside ourselves and send spiritual messages outward. As is often said, we are spiritual beings here to have a physical experience. Empathy is a vital pathway for continually transforming our physical experiences into the spiritual lessons they are.

Empathic Abilities as Spiritual Gifts

Nearly every religion and culture emphasizes our spiritual nature. We are spiritual beings that travel the universe through our souls; our body is a temple for these heavenly based aspects of ourselves. Our spiritual gifts are the conduits that link the very spiritual elements of our true being with the concrete and grounded aspects of our material nature.

A variety of terms are used to describe the spiritual gifts. These include psychism, intuition, mysticism, subtle abilities, ESP, the supernatural, the paranormal, the sixth sense, and energetic abilities. Of these, I really like the last term because it explains how we are able to tune in to situations, people, objects, and celestial forces—and past, present, and future—in inexplicable ways. We do so energetically. We can sense what is beyond our ordinary five senses because we are made of energy.

Energy is simply information that moves. Everything inside 3-D reality is made of energy. Your phone? It's a phone because the information encoded within its molecular and energetic structure tells it to be a phone. The voices you hear over the phone? They are made of energy, or information, moving at a certain speed.

Beyond our common points of reference, there is a lot of energy that isn't as measurable as the weight of a phone or the sound of another's voice. This is the spiritual or psychic energy that we're able to tune in to through our spiritual gifts.

Of course, we receive and send a lot of messages through our typical five senses in any given moment. We gaze at the world through the lenses of our eyes. We hear the birds and crickets because our auditory system is able to tune in to these creatures. We look forward to a meal that smells tangy and pungent and will taste equally satisfying. And we know we are loved when someone strokes our hair or touches our skin in a certain way.

Our spiritual gifts, however, attune us to energy or information that lies outside the bounds of our five senses. Because of these gifts, we can access and track information that flies faster than the speed of light, which links us to people we've never met or bonds us with someone on the other side of the world—information that sometimes comes from a future we've yet to imagine. Our spiritual gifts enable us to gain intuitive insight from the Divine and know, for example, what it might be like to soar like a hawk or burrow like a rabbit.

Our spiritual gifts aren't separate from our sensory abilities. In fact, we wouldn't be able to hear God's whisper or receive a revelatory dream or just "know" when we're supposed to reach out to a friend if we weren't able to decipher the spiritual, subtle information through our bodies. Energy is energy. A thought is a thought. Reality does not divide cleanly in half—spiritual on one side, physical on the other. We need to understand that the two "halves" are merely interconnected ways of knowing along the same continuum. A biological equivalent to this is the information sharing that happens through the molecular structure of our DNA—the double helix.

In short, we are spiritual beings who must continually make spiritual energy more physical, and we are physical beings capable of spiritualizing our physical energy.

In many ways, we are a lot like computers. Our bodies are like compact and efficient 3-D laptops. They can receive and store data and retrieve it. But they are only going to pay attention to the information they are programmed to accept by their software.

Some of this information is entered manually, much as we type into a word processor. We can think of this as equivalent to using sensory-based energy or information. But some kinds of information simply appear, much like email or an instant message. This information, which we still inevitably need to decipher through our normal senses, is similar to psychic or spiritual energy. It moves faster and travels in ways that appear magical when we perceive it through our normal filters.

In a nutshell, our spiritual self can do instant messaging, while our physical self has to operate manually.

The Three Categories of Spiritual Gifts

As I indicated earlier, there are three main forms of spiritual gifts involved in empathy, the psychic mechanisms that do the instant messaging.

The first category is the bodily empathic gifts, through which empathy registers in us physically. There are five of these: clear sensing (clairsentience), which can manifest emotionally or mentally; clear tasting (clairgustance); clear smelling (clairscent); clear touching (clairtangency); and clear knowing (claircognizance).

The other two categories are clear seeing (clairvoyance) and clear hearing (clairaudience), each of which, as I explained in the introduction, I consider a set, or "family," of gifts because each can manifest in multiple forms. A person with the gift of clairvoyance, for example, might receive visions when awake or asleep, pictorial revelations, or imaginative images that provide insight and inspiration.

Every one of these gift families allows us to receive and share information that can go backward and forward in time, to know the seemingly unknowable, and to create change without lifting a finger.

Maybe you don't think you are gifted in any of these categories. Surprise! That's simply not true. We are all able to connect with spiritual or psychic information, although many of us don't always know we are doing so. Maybe you haven't been taught how to recognize or label this spiritual information, or perhaps it scares you, so you ignore it. Or you might live at the other side of the spectrum and feel constantly overwhelmed by spiritual information rather than blessed by it. In any case, we are all born with the ability to send, receive, decipher, and handle spiritual energy.

But there is a common misconception that leaves many people thinking they don't have any spiritual gifts because theirs fall into the bodily empathy category. Clairvoyance is an obvious spiritual gift; after all, clairvoyants perceive images that no one else can see. Throughout history, many a king and pauper alike have consulted clairvoyants—who were sometimes called oracles or diviners—to focus that inner sight on their own concerns. Clairvoyant images are still considered visions from the Divine, revelatory tools by which to steer one's life, and this gift is often portrayed in the popular media of the day.

Clairaudience also merits a lot of press time, even on television, though you may be less familiar with the term than with words that are more commonly used to describe people with this gift: mediums, transmediums, channelers, and people with the gift of telepathy. These people can read minds, talk to the dead, or deliver messages from the "other side."

These "glamorous" gifts often outshine their bodily cousins, whose grounded capabilities can sometimes seem mundane or pedantic in comparison with the high-flying images or insightful words that come through the clairvoyant or clairaudient gifts, respectively. Yet empathic ability, with all its subtlety, is no less important.

Empathy is fully dependent on our material bodies, as you will see when you dive into the next chapter. This means that by engaging empathically, we fully engage with the physical aspects of life. Empathy encourages bonding and thus promotes our ultimate spiritual purpose: to learn about love. And all forms of empathy invite us to move beyond our individual selves, promoting expansion beyond our limited egos and the stretch into higher consciousness.

In spiritual circles, however, the bodily empathic gifts aren't always seen as measuring up against the better-known clairvoyance and clairaudience, and this skewed viewpoint can make someone who has a rich experience of bodily empathy feel "less than." Until we get beyond this judgment, it will be difficult for us to fully access and develop our empathy, no matter which gifts are our strongest.

All Spiritual Gifts Are Created Equal

Many of the empaths I meet feel confused or even apologetic that they are not clairvoyant or clairaudient. Even individuals with all three gifts can seem underwhelmed by their bodily empathic abilities in comparison to their visual or verbal aptitudes. "Can't I just cut out my bodily empathic gifts and see pictures?" asked one of my intuition students. "It's so much easier."

I can relate to feeling at least a little jumbled and even slightly scornful, as I used to have this attitude myself. Bodily empathy often leaves us more perplexed than perceptive and more muddled than demystified. There is a simple reason for this: it can be hard to separate our empathic sensations from our personal reactions. In contrast, it's easier to visualize a psychic picture or hear an intuitive message and know that it doesn't originate within us.

For instance, think about the last time you were in a great mood—that is, before you started talking to someone who was irritated. You suddenly realized you were feeling irritated too, yet only now noticed that your mood had changed. You might not have connected your attitude change with what is truly a gift if recognized and developed: the ability to feel what someone else is experiencing.

The body that is sensing what another is going through is your own. It can be very hard to distinguish which bodily sensations, sensitivities, emotions, or perceptions originate inside you from those that started in someone (or something) else. Now perhaps you can understand why it seems easier and clearer to simply receive a picture or a message.

So empathic information can baffle us, causing self-doubt. It can also be harder to relay bodily empathic information than clairvoyant or clairaudient data. Plain and simple, it's more challenging to work with kinesthetic (sensed in the body) information than visual or verbal.

Imagine you are trying to tell your boss that his approach to a project isn't going to work (let's assume you're willing to risk saying anything at all). It doesn't sound very powerful to say "it doesn't feel right to me" or "your idea turns my stomach." Compare these to "I see this process going down in flames" or "if I could offer guidance, it would be to say that you should try a different method."

While the gifts of clairvoyance or clairaudience might seem more striking or dramatic, the body-based sensations of empathy showcase what is fundamentally human about us: our senses, feelings, consciousness, bonds, and knowledge. Foundationally, they assist us in being what we really are—divine beings exploring a human experience, the basis of which is love, or connection. And, of course, empathy joined with an image or a word only enhances our ability to understand what our clairvoyance or clairaudience is sharing with us.

Can there be a more loving act than to sense another's joy or despair, to know how they feel and what they need? To link with the worlds of nature and of spirit? To embrace another so completely that we become as if we are one with them? It is the kinesthetic kinship of empathy that allows us to bond with someone or something without losing ourselves in the process and invites what is arguably the most important quality in the universe: compassion.

In fact, it is in the name of compassion that you have been gifted with empathy, and your body is a perfect vehicle for the empathic experience. The empathic capacity of the human body is the subject of chapter 2.

CHAPTER 2

Your Empathic Body: Wired to Connect

And fear not lest Existence closing your
Account, and mine, should know the like no more;
The Eternal Saki from the Bowl has pour'd
Millions of Bubbles like us, and will pour.

THE RUBAIYAT OF OMAR KHAYYAM

Deep inside, many of us feel isolated and alone. We are encased by our skin, separated by experience, and wrapped within our uniqueness. But the very body that makes most of us feel individuated, and sometimes alienated, is biologically and energetically hardwired for connection.

Through special neurons and a spectrum of electromagnetic forces, we are equipped to relate to the many worlds around us—spheres of influence both visible and invisible. We are "coded" for empathy and designed to share information through nonphysical means. We are each a bubble in a bowl of sparkling liquid light, separate and yet reflective of every other facet of the universe.

Depending on which of the empathic gifts described in the last chapter are strongest in you, these special nerves and electromagnetic waves will attune you to different points of reference, and this will determine your empathic style. Are you wired for physicality or emotionality? Mentality or natural energies? Are you primarily spiritually aware? Or are you shamanically inclined, with many facets as your reference points? (You will learn the characteristics of all of these empathic styles in chapter 4.)

In this chapter I will take you on a journey through the body's wisdom—your body electric—so you can better understand your own personal empathic abilities and how they work. For all of us, knowing what is occurring inside ourselves is a key to better embracing and dealing with what is happening *outside* ourselves.

A Quick Journey into the Past

You have been handed a free ticket to Italy. You board the plane and notice that it isn't like any old aircraft: this one is designed for time travel.

Almost instantaneously, you are transported into a research laboratory. You have been invited to observe what has become a critical experiment that will lead to greater understanding of empathy and connection.

The scientists in this room are studying the behavior of macaque monkeys. They have already figured out that when a monkey performs a certain hand action, the neurons in its motor cortex show extreme activity. For instance, you can observe a monkey as it reaches for a peanut and watch for the resulting fireworks. Cells on either side of the monkey's brain fire, creating a buzzing sound that is audible on the monitoring equipment.

You are present on a very important day. Today one of the scientists gets hungry and grabs a peanut for himself. A monkey watches as the scientist reaches for the nut, and the nerves in the monkey's brain fire as if it were reaching for the peanut, not the scientist. The monkey's cells cannot tell the difference between watching something being done and doing it themselves.[1]

As you return home via your time-travel airplane, you reflect on the consequences of this discovery. If merely observing an activity is equal to performing it, a person can learn how to do something by watching. You can watch a golf program and boost your golf swing or observe a loving couple and learn how to become more caring in your own relationships. Even more importantly, you can relate to what is occurring in people or other influences outside yourself; in fact, their experiences become your own.

The experiment you have just read about really happened in 1992, and the scientists' observations formed the basis for our contemporary scientific understanding of empathy. Since our monkey friends revealed their empathic abilities, we have named the special nerve cells that enable empathy *mirror neurons,* an appropriate label for nerves that allow us to mirror others' activities. These mirror neurons help us do more than learn and further develop, however; they also reflect sensations and feelings.

Our mirror neurons could be called *empathy neurons,* and they are part of an intricate and beautiful process whereby we can live as the empathic beings we are. It is these nerves that we must comprehend in order to understand the physical basis of our spiritual empathic gifts.

Your Empathic Body

Because we have these mirror neurons, we can duplicate the emotional or sensory state of another's mind and body. What's happening in someone else gets transferred into us as if we are having the same experience. Researchers looking into this have produced some fascinating results.

For instance, researchers monitored what happened when one human subject watched another one wave his hand, first in a caressing gesture and then more rudely. Neither wave was directed toward the observer, yet over the course of multiple pairings and repetitions, the brains of the people watching the rude wave registered the same level of shock as if they themselves were on the receiving end of it.[2]

This process is sometimes called parallel circuitry, meaning that our reactions run parallel to what someone else is experiencing, doing, or feeling. The particular nerves making up this circuitry act like a sort of neural Wi-Fi that monitors what's going on in others. Through this Wi-Fi of mirror neurons, we can unconsciously and instantaneously assess another's feelings, movements, and even intentions.

Emotional intelligence expert Daniel Goleman compares this wiring to a sort of social brain—an apt term for a system that enables us to sense what is occurring in others.[3] It is an automatic system, always "turned on," even though studies suggest that it is most active when we are paying attention to an activity rather than observing it passively. *This means that we might be most empathic when we are* trying *to be empathic.*[4] An important follow-on is that we can activate empathy *within ourselves.* So if for any reason our empathic abilities are repressed or impaired, we can consciously choose to mature into empathic beings who can serve self and others with love and compassion.

A Brief Dive into the Biochemistry of Empathy

In your quest to better understand the role of your energetic body in your empathic experience, it can be very helpful to acquaint yourself with the biochemistry at work. Our mirror neurons aren't the only biological factor involved in creating empathy. Other key components include parts of our brain and certain endocrine functions. It has become increasingly clear that there are particular brain states that enhance empathy and others that limit it. For example, research at the University of Wisconsin reveals that compassion meditation, a form of Buddhist meditation, seems to increase empathy.

The Wisconsin researchers combined expert and novice meditation students and exposed them all to sounds that stimulated their emotions, both positive and negative. They discovered that all of these emotional sounds caused the students' pupils to widen and activated the limbic sections of the brain—the parts involving the urge to fight, flee, or freeze. Other parts of the brain associated with survival reactions responded as well. In general, however, advanced meditators reacted more to negative emotional stimulation than did novices, and they strove to make a positive difference as well. All of this in reaction to only sound!

Overall, the researchers concluded that empathy is highly geared toward our emotional and fight-or-flight systems and appears to be innate. While meditation can increase a person's empathic reactions, all the subjects in this study seemed able to react to emotional triggers simply because our brains are wired for it.[5]

Other studies suggest that our mirror neurons, brains, and endocrine systems work together to create a bodily matrix that invites empathy and compassion. Put another way, because endocrine glands are distributed throughout the body, our entire body is an empathic tool. A thrilling scientific paper called "Rewarding Altruism" by Mariana Lozada, Paola D'Adamo, and Miguel Angel Fuentes examines studies from several disciplines that support this idea.[6]

One conclusion this paper reached was that the human body is a complex tapestry oriented toward both empathy and one of its potential effects: altruism, the act of doing good simply to do good. Altruism and compassion are kissing cousins in that both lead to a loving social order and kind interactions. In a sense, we could say that altruism is compassion in action. The shaping of empathy into the end goal of altruism, however, takes all three biological systems (nerves, parts of the brain, and endocrine functions) acting in concert.

What is especially exciting is the discovery that not every component of empathy is based in the brain. Yes, our mirror neurons and emotion-related brain parts are located in our head, but hormones and neuropeptides travel throughout the body, carried in our bloodstream and with other bodily fluids. Thus far, science has identified more than ninety neuropeptides that help regulate our moods in addition to performing other functions such as calibrating our blood pressure and monitoring our immune system.[7] Yet other peptides, or protein chains, that form hormones are directly responsible for love and bonding.

Three of the most important hormones necessary for bonding—a critical aspect of empathy and the resulting choice to be compassionate or altruistic—include oxytocin, dopamine, and serotonin. Oxytocin, often called the "love hormone," actually increases when we are cooperating with others. This hormone is produced in the brain and released by the pituitary gland, but science has also found oxytocin in the heart, along with oxytocin receptors.[8] A peptide made by nine amino acids, oxytocin strengthens social behaviors, bonding members of a group together. It bolsters our ability to approach another person with care and concern and invites helping behavior.

One study even showed that administering oxytocin to people prompted them to make more cash donations![9] Yet another revealed it as a potentially effective treatment for many symptoms of autism, such as difficulties in talking and repetitive behaviors, even while it increased emotional connectivity in people with autism.[10] Along these same lines, both dopamine and serotonin, two other important bonding hormones, promote (and can result from) cooperative behavior in individuals as well as social cooperation.[11]

As exciting as it is to recognize the fact that our bodies are intricately coded for empathy, another important conclusion we can draw from the "Rewarding Altruism" study is that following through on empathy is actually good for us. As several studies have revealed, acting empathically—being altruistic and compassionate—actually reduces our own stress.

It seems that when we empathically recognize stress in another person and seek to alleviate it, our own stress hormones decrease. Our immune system is enhanced, and we enjoy fewer and less severe viral infections, better heart rates, lower blood pressure, lower counts of serum cholesterol, and other important indicators of good health. Effective empathy—taking positive actions based on our empathic perceptions—has nothing but beneficial effects on stress levels, immunity, and life expectancy.

EMPATHIC EXPLORATION 2 *What Do You Feel in Your Body?*

Because we are all physically wired for empathy, we've all had the experiences of empathy in our bodies. You might have felt another's emotions, needs, or awareness in your abdomen—or nose, toes, or heart. Take a few moments and reflect on the last time you sensed what was occurring with someone (or something) else. In what part of your body did you feel that empathic information? Did it feel warm, cool, heavy, light, or just different? What caused you to notice it? Does this experience tell you anything about yourself?

The Social Contract: Why We Are Wired "Just So"

While it's obvious that we are wired for empathy and even the higher forms of love including compassion (as you'll see in chapter 3), we might still ask why.

Why *are* we wired for what might be called "interactive love"?

Most social researchers believe empathy assures both personal and tribal survival. This makes sense when we look at the reasons that adults are programmed for empathy. Because of empathy, we take care of our children, help our loved ones, and save those who need to be saved. But recent research reveals that we are programmed *from birth* to help our family members. In fact, infants display altruistic behavior, providing comfort, information, and assistance to family members. That's right: babies will reach out when their moms or dads are in distress.

At first glance, this empathic gesturing is logical enough. Our parents are our original kin. Perhaps we're encoded to care for them so that they will care for us in return. But even young children are quite capable of being empathic and altruistic to those outside their families as well. Experiments show that children between the ages of one and two will share their favorite toys or other objects with both familiar and unfamiliar individuals, and that older children, those between six and ten, prefer cooperative rather than competitive games.[12]

Are we coded toward empathy simply because getting along rewards us? No; we are designed for kindness for reasons beyond survival and selfishness. In fact, one study shows that twenty-month-old children are more likely to be altruistic when they do *not* get a material reward for being kind.[13]

Scientific and anecdotal evidence alike indicates that within the human spirit is the compulsion to be kind just for its own sake. Our empathic wiring is secondary to this inner compelling quality.

There are a lot of reasons a person might not develop empathy, however, or why their empathic and compassionate actions might be distorted (for more on this, see appendix 2 on impaired empaths). At this point, we want to underline the exciting news that we are encoded with a sort of innate and primal programming for goodness, starting with empathy.

Our bodies are only one mechanism for empathic sharing, however. There is another "body" besides our physical one, called the energy body, or our energetic anatomy. To fully understand the pathways used for transferring information from one person to another, we must receive a short lesson in energetics.

The Body Electric—and Magnetic: How We Transfer Energy

While empathy requires healthy interaction between our neurological, brain, and endocrine functions, it involves more than a biochemical series of mirror neuron bleeps, brain starbursts, and hormonal rushes. It also relies on our body's energetic anatomy, a set of energy-based systems that interconnect our spirit and our physical body.

Our energetic systems—namely our energy fields, chakras, and meridians—are capable of transferring physical or sensory energy into spiritual energy, also called subtle, or psychic, energies. These systems also perform in the reverse, transforming psychic energy into physical energy.

Sneaky, sly, slippery, and shimmery, energy transfers from one place to another because we are energetic beings. In fact, in terms of what is now scientifically knowable, energy is the basis of every living and nonliving thing.

One of the reasons empaths can sense what is occurring in people, places, or beings in other time zones, locations, and spaces is that their energetic fields extend way beyond their physical body.

Let's explore this in personal terms.

Your most basic energetic field is called your electromagnetic field, or EMF. Yet your EMF is actually not a single field. It comprises the electrical and magnetic energies emanating from the atoms, molecules, cells, and organs that make up your physical self. Every aspect of your body emanates, shares, and generates electricity. You are a body electric—in some ways, a gigantic light bulb. Electricity, in turn, creates magnetic fields. The electrical charges and the resulting magnetic fields combine to create your overall EMF.

Your heart generates your body's most expansive and far-reaching EMF. Your heart's electrical field is about sixty times greater in amplitude than that of your brain, and its magnetic field, as compared to your brain, is nearly five thousand times stronger.[14] This field extends at least three feet beyond your physical body, and it interacts with the cognitive functions of those in your vicinity to such an extent that the pattern of your own heart's frequencies can be perceived by another person's brain. Information about your emotional state is especially strong, and the people near you can often perceive it. Peer-reviewed research from the Institute of HeartMath reveals that in addition to emotions, we also transmit coded information such as our thoughts and needs and even our states of wellness or disease.[15]

Empathic people are aware of this energetic exchange. They know that they share information with people, beings, and objects that are more than three feet away and events that take place farther away than that. Physics explains this phenomenon to a certain extent with a theory called quantum entanglement. According to this theory, quanta are subatomic particles that can coexist in more than one place at a time, as well as travel outside the normal space-time continuum. "Entanglement" refers to the idea that once two particles, people, or objects have connected, they are forever linked, no matter where—or when—they are. People who believe in past lives could also assert that anything or anyone we have *ever* known is eternally linked to us.

In fact, science can now support this theory through studies proving that once two particles are entangled, they remain connected long after being separated. Activity in one particle produces identical change in the other, suggesting a slant on empathy. If two particles can identify with each other, even over a distance, so can two people (or a person and an animal, rock, or object). But the effects of entanglement are even more bizarrely intimate.

Scientists have also made discoveries concerning entanglement that push the boundaries of our usual understanding of time, finding that particles that are no longer bonded can still remain entangled. This phenomenon, which Einstein referred to as "spooky action at a distance," suggests that future actions can influence past events.[16] For instance, two people can potentially meet "in the future" and then draw themselves to each other in the present.

Yet another theory can add to our understanding of across-time-and-space connections. Experiments have also shown that we can share information from one person's (or being's) EMF to another, thus transferring information as if handing off a baton in a relay race. One researcher proposing this theory was Dr. Vlail Kaznacheyev, a Russian scientist who spent twenty years experimenting with EMFs. He discovered that biophotons—miniwave particles of light—can carry information from one body-field (another way of referring to a body's EMF) to another in a period of about forty-eight hours. His experiments also revealed that viruses and stress can (empathically) spread from one person to another. In all, he carried out twelve thousand experiments to sustain his theory that our body-fields can link us with others as if we're all part of a giant puzzle.[17]

I think it's important to point out that one of the reasons we are largely unaware of this interconnectivity is that we only perceive a glimmer of reality through our physical senses. Our eyes, for instance, can only perceive the visible fraction of the electromagnetic light spectrum, or light, which is less than 2 percent of the entire spectrum.[18] This means that when we are looking at something or someone, we are only noticing the relatively solid surface of that person or object, not what is occurring underneath—or what is emanating from them. We are, most likely, nothing more or less than oscillating fields of light: energy that is elegantly unencumbered. Blink and you've connected with someone—or somewhere—else. Blink again and they have sent you a message, and you, a message to them.

Auric Layers, Chakras, and Meridians: Other Energy Conduits

There is a special set of EMFs that extends at least thirty feet beyond our body, as well as into otherworldly arenas and realms. These are called the auric layers, and they are part of the auric field.

Various esoteric experts and practitioners believe we have anywhere from seven to twelve auric layers; I ascribe to the latter theory. Each layer protects us and filters different types of information while transmitting particular data to the world around us. (See figure, next page.)

I believe that each of these auric fields is an extension of another set of energetic bodies, called chakras. Seven of our chakras are based in the body, each linked with a specific endocrine gland and section of our spine. I work with a system that locates an additional five chakras outside the physical body.

Chakras look like spinning vortices of light. I envision these swirling waves of energy as forming the auric layers, each chakra creating its own sister field around the body. Each chakra and affiliated auric field runs on its own unique spectrum, or vibration, of energy and governs a specific set of concerns. Basically, the chakras hold our programs and issues, and our auric layers communicate them to the world.

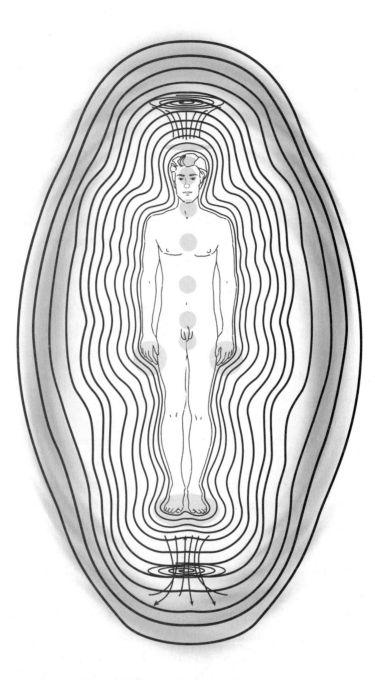

Figure: The Twelve Chakras and Auric Layers
This diagram exhibits the twelve chakras (indicated with shaded circles) and their corresponding auric layers surrounding the body. Each of the twelve chakras features a set of psychic abilities.

Complementing this effort is one more energetic system, described as meridians in Asian medicine systems and nadis in the Hindu system. The meridians are rivers or channels of energy that flow through the body, delivering subtle energy to all parts of it. They run through the chakras as part of their courseway, thus dropping and picking up energy that will be shared between all chakras and, through them, the auric layers.

More detailed information follows.

The Subtle Anatomy: Chakras and Auric Fields as Part of the Empathy Equation

Chakras are energy organs that convert sensory information into subtle energy and vice versa. They and their partners, the auric layers, comprise a rich resource for picking up and sending empathic information.

As I indicated, I work with a twelve-chakra system. Each of these twelve chakras connects into the body through an endocrine organ. The seven in-body chakras also link into the spine. Each chakra is a band of swirling energy that emanates in front and back of you, and also in a horizontal band around you.

Every chakra regulates a certain part of your body in addition to specific emotional, mental, relational, spiritual, and intuitive faculties. Each one will attract the information that suits it best, not only from people but also from other living and sentient beings. Some chakras also attune to events, spiritual issues, or otherworldly concerns, while others are most responsive to verbal or visual messages. Because chakric function isn't restricted to the here and now, they serve as antennae connecting to information as far-flung as other time periods, parallel or concurrent realities, potential futures, or even the tiny changes occurring in someone who is a thousand miles away.

One of the mechanisms for this receptivity, and for the radiant empathy capability of sending energy (described in chapter 4), is the auric field, which consists of twelve auric layers, each linked with one of the twelve chakras. Just as we are surrounded by a series of electromagnetic fields, so do pulsating and encircling bands of light encompass us.

Essentially, each chakra is partnered with a corresponding auric layer. For instance, chakra one (in the hip and pelvic area) interacts with the first auric field, which is in and just outside the skin. Chakra two is linked with the second auric field, and so on. Instead of imagining the chakras as separate but connected to their fellow auric layer, think of them as made of the same skein of yarn or bolt of cloth. The somewhat condensed energy of an in- or out-of-body chakra flows over the body and forms its auric kin. This means that what occurs in the auric field is registered also in its related chakra, and vice versa.

As I mentioned before, the auric field extends up to thirty feet or more beyond the body, but its reach is nearly infinite. Its oscillating waves of subtle energy can stretch as far as the skies and seas and flow right through the body of a snail or a blade of grass on the other side of the world. Free to touch any corner of the cosmos, these waves are not limited to the here and now either. Past, present, and future are all mere way stations for these traveling fields.

Through its related auric field, a chakra will receive the type of information that matches it, and an auric field will let in (or out) the energy it is programmed to work with. If our first chakra is programmed to receive information about others' physical well-being, the first auric layer will let in that information, thus creating a physical experience of empathy. If our second chakra is coded to attune to others' emotions, our second auric layer will respond, and we will experience emotional empathy.

Following is a list of the twelve chakras along with a brief explanation of the type of information each can receive or send. Also listed are the empathic styles that frequently relate to different chakras and the types of psychic abilities (the clairs) that often relate to them. These six styles will be more thoroughly discussed in chapter 4, where you'll have the opportunity to explore which empathic style most closely matches your experience, so make sure to flag this chart to refer back to later.

CHAKRA	LOCATION	TYPE OF INFORMATION	EMPATHIC STYLE	ASSOCIATED CLAIR ABILITIES
first	hips	physical and material	physical	clairgustance, clairscentience, and clairtangency
second	abdomen	emotional and creative	emotional	clairsentience
third	solar plexus	mental and informational	mental	clairsentience and claircognizance
fourth	heart	relational and healing	because it is relational, possibly all empathic styles and clair abilities	
fifth	throat	educational and verbal	mental	clairaudience
sixth	forehead	visual and futuristic	mental	clairvoyance
seventh	top of head	spiritual	spiritual	clairsentience and claircognizance
eighth	1½ inches over the head	mystical	shamanic	all clair abilities (shamans can also access all other chakras)
ninth	arm's length over the head	soul based	spiritual	clairsentience and clairaudience
tenth	1½ feet underground	environmental and nature based	natural	clairgustance, clairscentience, and clairtangency
eleventh	around body	natural and supernatural	natural and physical	clairsentience and claircognizance
twelfth		the twelfth chakra interpenetrates the twelfth auric field and surrounds our other auric fields; it is a boundary for our entire self and reflects our individuality		

Even Animals and Plants Have Empathic Bodies…
and They May Be Compassionate Too

Empathy is so often described in relation to people that we sometimes forget to ask the question: can animals or plants be empathic, maybe even compassionate?

Many empaths know that the answer to both is yes. Because they are able to sense the emotions of animals and other living beings—as well as plants, trees, and even natural, cosmic, and supernatural energies—their knowing is unequivocal. This certainty is only strengthened when they also feel the objects of their empathy respond. In fact, anyone who has ever been blessed with a loving companion animal knows that many animals can be compassionately empathetic. Within my own home, my son Gabriel, from age four onward, was the beloved human brother of two very unique dogs: Coco, a deaf and blind chocolate Lab we received after she was abandoned on a highway, and Honey, a golden retriever we raised from puppyhood.

Every time Gabe was upset, Honey would sit near him and lick his face. In fact, Honey then followed Gabe around the house, licking as he went, until Gabe felt better. Coco would lie at Gabe's feet and refuse to budge until Gabe stopped crying. Honey and Coco have died, but we are currently watched over by a gigantic yellow Labrador named Lucky, who goes a step further than his predecessors. If Gabe is worried, Lucky will not only sit near him but directly *on* him, all ninety pounds of him engaged in assuring that Gabe either feel better fast or be squished.

I hear stories like these from all over the world, some of which have appeared in the news. Recently, a mother of two from Britain discovered how genuine animal empathy is after figuring out that there was a reason her cat, Fidge, kept jumping on her breast for weeks on end. Fidge's "mom" finally went to the doctor, who discovered a malignant tumor that would have metastasized if it hadn't been found.

Joining the circle "in the know" are hundreds of scientists, especially those focused on neuroscience and psychology, who are merging into the burgeoning field called neuroethology, or the study of animal behavior resulting from neurological codes. The field has expanded to suggest that animals might be coded for empathy the same way humans are, specifically through mirror neurons and the fear centers of the brain.

According to a review of several studies published in *Scientific American*, researcher Dale J. Langford and his colleagues at McGill University showed that empathy in animals isn't limited to our companion animals but also includes mice.

In one particular study, two mice were placed in transparent tubes. They could not touch, but they could see each other. One mouse was injected with a solvent that caused a stomachache and obvious signs of discomfort, such as writhing. Researchers discovered that the noninjected mouse would writhe in reaction to the mouse in pain—but only if the two mice had originally been companions, indicating that a previous relationship was fundamental to the empathic sensing of pain. Additional aspects of the study showed that the mice were not merely imitating; each was actually sensing what the other mouse was going through and reacting accordingly.[19]

Would a mouse rescue another mouse, as certain animal companions or humans might seek to do? One recent study suggests that they might—or that rats would, at least. The lead author of one particular study, Peggy Mason of the Department of Neurobiology at the University of Chicago, showed that rats will liberate trapped cage mates even when they have nothing to gain. All the female rats tested opened doors for their companions, while only 70 percent of the male rats did.[20]

While we can't prove that animals necessarily feel what other animals are going through, the results of these studies suggest that animals at least observe and react to another's emotional state, most likely for some of the same reasons humans are equipped with empathy. Humans and other animals have a better chance at surviving threats when they can sense each other's pain. When we see others who are suffering, injured, or hurting, we are then compelled to care for them.[21]

If animals are potentially hardwired for empathy, how about plants, some of our other planetary neighbors? Several fascinating studies show that plants react when injured or damaged, but one set of experiments stands out in particular.

Cleve Backster is one of the granddaddies of experimentation with plant empathy. An American specialist in lie detection, Backster conducted research on more than thirty different types of plants in order to prove his hypothesis that plants are wired for empathetic reactions.

Backster used a lie detector for most of his experiments, attaching electrodes to the plants. A lie detector measures a human subject's reaction as an erratic wave on the machine's graph paper. This wave is a response to a galvanic skin reflex (GSR). Backster was searching for similar reactions from plants, believing that the plant could detect an emotional response in another organism.

Not only was Backster able to identify changes in the lie detectors when the plants were actually threatened, but changes showed up even when he *thought about* threatening them. Yet when he merely pretended that he was going to threaten a plant, the plant "played possum" and didn't respond. Backster concluded that plants, like people (and possums), have their own form of empathic ESP and natural intelligence.[22]

In a different experiment, researchers threw several batches of live brine shrimp into boiling water at intermittent times. The researcher in charge of reading the lie detectors hooked to the plants had no idea when these different batches of shrimp were being killed. Each time a batch was killed, the plants responded with a GSR reading similar to that shown in a human being when under stress.[23]

Backster's conclusion to this and other experiments was to assert that plants react to many external factors, including emotions felt by humans, the presence of humans, and movements in the environment. In fact, as I've already alluded to, they often react before something has occurred.

Distance didn't always seem to be a factor either, at least not when there was a long-standing association between a plant and a person. Backster once asked a friend to send love to her plants when she was seven hundred miles away, focusing most of her loving attention on one in particular. They synchronized wristwatches in order to track the plant's responses and discovered that it reacted every time the owner sent love. Interestingly, the plant also responded to the anxiety she felt when her plane touched down at her destination.[24]

Several Russian researchers took Backster's discoveries a step further, citing their own research in a little-known book called *Parapsychology and Contemporary Science*.[25] In their book, researchers Dubrove and Pushkin acknowledged others' research showing that plant cells placed in separate test tubes can communicate with each other, thus revealing an empathy between living cells.

In their own psychobotanical research, Dubrove and Pushkin used an electroencephalograph in contrast to Backster's electrical measurements but quickly discovered that not all human subjects could elicit a response in plants. To equalize the humans' capacity for sending emotional energy, they used hypnosis, thus initiating all subjects into a similar mental state.

The reactions of the plants to human emotions now became much more consistent, but not completely so. The Russian researchers found that the more emotional and temperamental the human subject, the more responsive the plants were to both positive and negative emotions.

These sorts of studies suggest that more than humans and animals can be empathic, if not compassionate, and another interesting experiment takes us a step further. A research project at Keio University in Japan did more than simply measure plants' reactions; rather, it aimed at helping living plants react directly to what people are thinking and feeling. In other words, they sought to *teach* plants how to relate to humans.

The researchers created a complex system for fashioning these "interactive plants" so they could respond to a person's emotions by attaching each plant to a microphone and a motion sensor. When humans made specific movements that conveyed emotions, the plants physically moved, seemingly with empathy. One of the long-range goals of the research is to actually train plants to meet humans' needs. Maybe a guardian cactus outside our door that alerts us to a threat? Or a tender fern that soothes us after a stressful day at work?[26]

The fact that plants, animals, and humans share the empathic sense suggests that we really are all part of a global family. While our bodily and energetic systems are more complex than those of our nature-based kin, every life form is engaged in sharing information and creating a harmonic net of compassion, the subject of chapter 3.

CHAPTER 3

Compassion: The Lining of the Empath's Soul

*If we have no peace, it is because we have
forgotten that we belong to each other.*

MOTHER TERESA

By now you are gaining a good understanding of the wide range of extraordinary gifts we all possess that foster connection—both the subtle, psychic empathic gifts and the gifts within our bodies, our physical wiring for empathy. Perhaps the single most important reason to develop and utilize these gifts is that they lead us swiftly and directly to compassion, the call to ease another's suffering. If there is anything we need in this world right now, it's compassion. Yet is there anything that is so little rewarded in our fast-paced, success-oriented world?

While all of us are wired for empathy, not all empaths are compassionate, moved to act on their empathic experiences. While the fledgling empath can receive meaningful signals and impressions without being moved to uplift someone else with those energetic messages, mature empathy always results in compassion. As we shall explore in this chapter, an innate empath is someone who can sense what is really happening outside themselves. And the soul of an empath is designed to take the next crucial step: to make a difference based on the empathic information they naturally pick up.

There is a Buddhist story that ends with this moral: "Truth, wholesomeness, and compassion can save the world."[27]

A Crisis of Compassion Is at Hand

Think of what the world—or even a small part of it—might look like without compassion, the highest goal of empathy.

A client of mine, Aaron, didn't have to imagine it; he was living it. Suddenly he'd had a disturbing epiphany: he realized that he had lost touch with the compassionate person he had once been. He had come to me to see if I could help him find that person again.

"When I was younger, I was the most empathic kid around," he told me. "I was the kid who found the stray cats and wounded birds and nursed them back to health. I could always tell when my mom was upset and needed cheering up. I even knew when the weather was going to change and I'd tell my dad, who was a farmer, so he could prepare. He called me his 'human almanac.'"

Aaron paused before tearing up. "But somewhere along the line, I decided it was more important to just get ahead. I decided that being myself wasn't enough. I decided it was safer to be absent, even from myself."

After another quiet moment, he added, "Do you think I can ever become compassionate again?"

The values underlying empathy, including compassion, kindness, and care, are on the wane. These "feeling muscles," which give strength to our humanity, are atrophied and aching, something Aaron astutely recognized within his own being. The Western world is experiencing an epidemic of loneliness, depression, and anxiety. A recent survey conducted by the University of Arizona and Duke University and incorporating data from the General Social Survey (GSS) showed that the number of Americans who state that they have *no one* with whom to discuss important matters tripled between 1985 and 2004. In fact, 25 percent of all Americans believe that they have no one with whom they can share a problem.[28] This changing (and some might say sagging) social support is one of the reasons, many researchers believe, stress is taking such a huge toll on our health.

As psychologists Ed Diener and Martin Seligman have shown, social connectedness predicts a longer life, quicker recovery from disease, higher levels of happiness, and the sense of a purposeful life. And according to a large-scale study, people lacking interaction are more vulnerable to disease and death than those who exhibit traditional high-risk behaviors such as smoking, hypertension, obesity, and lack of exercise.[29] Despite the fact that we would be healthier and happier if we bonded—if we used our empathic abilities and acted on them—we do not. And we are suffering because of it.

So extreme is the situation that expert Douglas LaBier, a business psychologist and director of the Center for Progressive Development, has coined the term "empathy deficit disorder," or EDD. While you won't find this term in the psychiatric diagnostic manuals, LaBier—along with many other socially aware individuals—believes that it is real and that it applies to our entire culture. As he points out, it is possible for an entire culture to share a mental pathology. And because it becomes the norm, it is difficult to spot or define.

According to LaBier, EDD is reflected in our inability to step outside ourselves and tune in to others' experiences, especially those who differ from us in feeling and belief. This is the primary source of personal conflicts, breakdowns in intimate relationships, and such adversarial attitudes as prejudice and discrimination between groups of people.

LaBier sees EDD mirrored in patterns of selfishness in relationships, such as when a spouse won't help his mate because he "needs" his "free time." In America, the epidemic of EDD is apparent in the discrimination against the religion of Islam and the assumption that every Muslim is a potential terrorist. But he also sees EDD playing out globally, visible in warfare between groups, clans, and societies with differing beliefs.

What causes EDD? LaBier indicates that it's our individual and collective inability to empathize with others—to get a glimpse of others through *their* lens, not only our own, and to see and value others as they are rather than who we want them to be.

As you learned in the last chapter, empathy is hardwired in each of us, but we have to choose to develop and use it.[30] The fact that being empathic—and compassionate—improves our own health should be enough to sell us on developing these skills. The Dalai Lama coyly asserts, "If we say, oh, the practice of compassion is something holy, nobody will listen. If we say, warm-heartedness really reduces your blood pressure, your anxiety, your stress, and improves your health, people will listen."[31] But I believe that the real reason to develop our empathy and its behavioral result, compassion, shouldn't be as utilitarian or simplistic as "it's good for us." Compassionate empathy should be our goal because of its inherent *goodness*.

Fundamentally, compassion is a spiritual quality. It is the basis for most religious and spiritual expressions. While it might be good for our health and relationships, the essence of compassion is also the root of our spiritual heritage.

The Spiritual Call to Compassionate Empathy Across Traditions

Compassion arises when an empath acts altruistically, choosing to alleviate the suffering of another simply because it's the right thing to do. As it ought to be, compassion is considered one of the greatest of virtues in nearly every religion, one we are called to cultivate and demonstrate.

In Judaism, God is known as the Compassionate Father who constantly exhibits the desire to relieve suffering or show mercy. The Hebrew word for "compassionate" is *rahmana,* which is also the designation for God's revealed word. To follow God's word is to do as God does: to be compassionate and loving. To do the opposite, to be cruel, is deplorable. Shares one of the great rabbis from the first century, Rabbi Hillel the Elder, "That which is hateful to you, do not do to your fellow. That is the whole Torah. The rest is the explanation."[32]

In Christianity, Jesus embodies the essence of relational compassion, taking the wounds of the world upon himself, even into death, so that they might be healed. His dedication to compassion, to selfless action, is unarguable. Although many Christian sects don't adhere to the essence of his words or live out his legacy of kindness, Jesus was clear that compassionate empathy should cross secular and religious lines.

An example of Jesus's intense belief in compassion is clearly demonstrated in his telling of the parable of the Good Samaritan, offered in Luke 10:25–37. According to Jesus's story, a Samaritan is traveling. This non-Jewish man is a member of a sect the Jews despise and degrade. Despite the fact that they consider him dirty and filthy, the Samaritan assists a traveler—who might himself be Jewish—who has been beaten, robbed, and left for dead. A priest and a Levite, holy men who "should" do the right thing, have already ignored this injured journeyer. As Jesus points out, the "way to heaven" is to act as did the Samaritan, who took it upon himself to show mercy to another even though he would reap no reward for it.

Among Muslims, compassion is one of the most important qualities a person can strive for. Muslim scripture urges not only that we care, but that we *act* in caring ways toward captives, widows, orphans, and the poor. Looking within ourselves, we can see that these people exist inside us in personal ways; each of us has felt trapped, lost, and bereft at times in our lives. Looking outwardly, one of the reasons Muslims fast during the month of Ramadan is to increase their ability to empathize with the hunger pangs of the less fortunate, to become more sensitive to others' plights, and to develop compassion for those trapped in poverty.[33]

Compassion is also one of the central tenets of Buddhism. It was Buddha who said the following: "Compassion is that which makes the heart of the good move at the pain of others. It crushes and destroys the pain of others; thus, it is called compassion."[34]

And as the Dalai Lama has said, "If you want others to be happy, practice compassion. If you want to be happy, practice compassion."

In Buddhism, this desire for loving-kindness in action is extended to all living beings, not only people. What is the key to achieving the highest level of all, compassion? As American monk Bhikkhu Bodhi describes it, it involves entering the subjective state of others to share their feelings and their interior space in every way.[35] In other words, it is to be empathetic to such a level that you become the other.

This Buddhist ideal reminds me of Jesus's Golden Rule. We are to love another as we love ourselves. How can we not love another if we *are* the other?

In Hinduism, compassion has its own name—*daya*—and is one of three central virtues. We've only to read the most ancient of Hindu scriptures, the Vedas, to find that it was considered deplorable to cause suffering to others and that it is important to refrain from causing harm.

We could search the world over and be hard pressed to find a religion that doesn't underscore the necessity and beauty of compassion.

What Does a Compassionate Empathic Experience Look Like?

If both empathy and compassion are so important, we might wonder what each of these qualities looks like, especially when joined together. How can we recognize them when they are present? Said in the shortest way possible, the equation for compassionate empathy is this: empathy moves us toward compassion.

Empathy, the first step involved in doing the "right thing," involves simply sensing what is occurring in something or someone else or relating to a situation that is outside ourselves. At other times, the entire experience is internal: we are compelled to empathize with ourselves or a part of ourselves. For example, when working with our inner child in the process of recovering from abuse or dealing with a personality or behavioral challenge, self-empathy gracefully opens the door to understanding, healing, and change.

To relate to someone is to sense what they are really going through. It involves entering their subjective experience and leaving behind the ideas and beliefs we might project on them or their situation.

For instance, you are empathizing with another person when you stop caring about your reactions to their pain and fully care about their pain instead. You are compassionately empathizing when you feel their joy at success instead of worrying about why you don't seem as successful. Likewise, empathy would include sharing in a friend's satisfaction in a job well done or pride in a decision well made. Your ability to do this tells the other person they can trust you to honor their needs, not simply project your own beliefs upon them. When you are able to fully sense another person or being, you can then sense what they need, not what you think they need. (In part II we will more fully discuss how this works in practice, and we will add the need to bring the Divine into the equation.)

It's easy to think that we are acting compassionately when we are simply acting out our own beliefs. One example of this is a man I'll call Max, one of my clients.

Max is the father of three sons. He came to see me because he was upset with his middle son, whom I will call Jimmy. Max's wife—the boys' mother—had died a few years earlier. While Max had never had a good relationship with Jimmy, the little that bonded them had deteriorated since the mother had died. In fact, Max was ready to kick fifteen-year-old Jimmy out of the house.

"All he does is defy me," the troubled father ranted. "He never does his homework, he is out until all hours of the night, and he is consistently rude to me."

I asked Max if he had ever tried to sense what was going on inside his son, not only observe from afar. Max had no idea what I was talking about.

"It's his job to figure out how to listen to *me*," Max bellowed. "After all, I know what's best."

Max truly thought he was doing what was best for his son by shouting at him and trying to discipline him with curfews, punishments, and restrictions. The problem was that he had failed to completely empathize with his son; he was only empathizing with his own hardship with his son.

As the middle child, Jimmy had been easily overlooked when his mother died. Max had been able to talk with his older son and cuddle with his youngest, but he didn't know how to get close to Jimmy. And so, conveniently, Max had assumed that Jimmy could figure how to deal with his mother's death on his own.

Complicating the scenario was the fact that Jimmy had attention deficit hyperactivity disorder (ADHD). His busy and impulsive behavior had always annoyed his staid and steady father, who believed that Jimmy was defying him when Jimmy was simply acting out his ADHD. Not only had Max failed to relate to his son with empathy, he hadn't spent the time he needed to truly observe his son and figure out his special needs.

It took several sessions for me to explain Jimmy to Max. At one point, Max even asked, "Why should I see things from my son's point of view? What makes him as important as me?" Max's empathic ability was obviously quite low, but it was evident that he did love his son. Eventually Max came to understand that Jimmy, given his special learning needs, was ill-prepared to deal with life. He was able to see that his son was lost and bereft rather than ill-behaved.

Gradually Max started to empathize with his son. He learned to use phrases like "I see what you mean" or "Can you help me understand why this is important to you?" As Max felt Jimmy's loss of a mother as Jimmy felt it, he was shocked to discover that one of the reasons Jimmy and he were so disconnected was that he had always left the parenting of Jimmy to his wife. Max vowed to spend more time alone with Jimmy, and he began to do so.

Max then took the next step and engaged a therapist, who worked with Jimmy to address his unresolved grief as well as his ADHD. Finally, Max got his son the scholastic help he needed, hiring a special coach to assist him with his learning challenges.

When Max first came to see me, he would have insisted that he was a compassionate man. He believed he was taking appropriate action to help his son. The problem was that he hadn't first empathized with Jimmy; he had never left his own world so he could enter that of his son. After learning how to sense Jimmy's real needs, Max broke through the compassion barrier and took actions that were truly for Jimmy's well-being.

As this story reveals, compassionate empathy requires more than loving intentions toward another person. It starts and ends with empathy. We must understand what another is going through within *their* frame of reference, not only our own. Only after we accomplish this initial goal can we broaden our minds and hearts and start to problem-solve.

Compassionate Empathy Toward the Self

As I suggested earlier, there are times when we must offer the same olive branch to ourselves. Most of us have unhealed "inner children" or even wounded "inner adults," parts of us that have been injured and left to suffer. Intertwined within the webbing of past events, these aspects of ourselves are essentially held hostage by pain. As we'll explore in this book, we might also be affected by past-life selves who are still traumatized by tragedy. We might even need to empathize with a current part of ourselves who is undergoing a relationship, work, or health challenge. As we all know, past or current dramatic experiences can lead to addictions, self-abuse, low self-esteem, financial difficulties, anxiety disorders, and countless other problems.

Most of us have learned to conceal our pain and trudge forward, acting as if we aren't hurt or suffering. We hide our injured selves and feelings inside a shell. Stuck within these nearly impenetrable walls, the wounded self only feels more scared, angry, hurt, or shameful as time goes on. Meanwhile, the remainder of our personality continues evolving until we forget about the part of ourselves that has been left bleeding and alone.

I have worked with numerous clients who have spent years in therapy trying to break down the barriers around the wounded parts of themselves. Many wonder why their everyday lives seldom improve, why patterns of abuse continue, and why they still don't believe themselves worthy of love, good health, or prosperity. One simple answer is that they are only working on their "today" self and not empathizing with their "yesterday" or "today" wounded self. They might also be forgetting that they could reach toward a future self who could empathically care for yesterday's and today's wounded selves.

Is a scared inner child going to leave her hiding place just because the adult self wants her to? Is an angry inner boy going to start trusting people just because his adult self insists he should? The key to healing ourselves is to empathize with the parts of us that are stuck in pain and drama.

By first identifying with our lost and lonely inner selves, we gain their trust. We let them know that we feel and care about their pain. We enter their world. By empathizing with them, we show them that they are not alone and that someone—our very self—understands why they feel the way that they do. Only after empathizing with these locked-away selves can we coax them out of their prisons.

Of course, we don't accomplish empathy by letting the wounded self take control of our lives. You wouldn't let an enraged three-year-old run around the house with a dangerous weapon, would you? Unfortunately, this is what often occurs, and it is likely one of the causes of narcissistic, borderline, abusive, and other challenging behaviors. Empathy might begin the process of self-healing, but compassionate action must complete it. It is compassionate to teach the inner three-year-old how to behave, not put them in charge of our lives. It is compassionate to provide discipline, comfort, and structure to the emerging wounded children within us, not give them permission to rule the roost and hurt other people simply because they are hurt. Compassionate behavior is, above all, responsible.

What Compassionate Empathy Isn't

Sometimes, in order to know what something is, you need to examine what it is not. We will further explore compassion, the lack of it, and other ways of being throughout this book, but I believe an early discussion about what empathy *is not* will be useful overall.

Compassionate empathy is many things. It is feeling, sensing, and caring. It is bonding, linking, and understanding. It includes acting, witnessing, and striving to make a difference. But it is not any of the following:

- sympathy/enmeshment
- personalizing
- imagination
- pity
- emotional contagion
- hyperoptimism
- mental maladjustment

Sympathy/Enmeshment

I think the most critical of these differentiations is that empathy is different from sympathy, and for people who want to delve further into this topic, I have included a lengthier discussion of this in appendix 1. There you will also find more discussion of the other things on the list that can masquerade as empathy.

When we empathize, we experience the thoughts, emotions, and direct experiences of another, an object, or a part of ourselves. We enter the other's subjective reality instead of simply observing their experience through our own so-called objective lens. Simultaneously, we are able to continue feeling our own reality. We don't lose ourself or forget our own senses, emotions, or needs simply because we are relating to someone else. In contrast, when we are sympathizing, we are so deeply experiencing the other's reality that we actually assume it. The result is that we lose contact with ourselves. The other's reality transplants our own. We become a secondary figure while the person, situation, or being we are sympathizing with becomes primary. We can even take on someone else's illnesses or conditions.

For instance, when I was a child, I had a dozen or so allergies. After I entered therapy as a client in my early twenties, my therapist suggested that I was carrying these allergies for my family members. She conducted a guided meditation in which I "returned" the allergies to their rightful owners. Within a few weeks, my family members started to complain of newly emerged allergies. Myself? I've only been afflicted with hay fever in the fall since then.

Yet another common example involves the sudden disappearance of your own reality and the just as immediate appearance of someone else's. How often have you experienced one of these events?

- You show up in a great mood for coffee with a friend. She's irritable. Within a few moments, you are angry and she is smiling.

- You are discussing a subject you're clear about with a loved one who disagrees with you and is mad because you won't budge. They "poke" at you until, finally, you explode. They walk away, smug. You've now relieved them of their frustration and, in fact, are even acting it out.

- You are ordering at a restaurant and your partner is taking forever; in fact, he or she seems to be creating a new dish. You can sense the waitperson's fear and frustration, and find yourself terrified. How are they going to get to their other customers? You are overidentifying with the waitperson.

Sympathy is reactionary. Rather than sensing another's reality and creating a bond, we go the extra step. We take on or even "fix" their discomfort by acting it out ourselves. This results in a smothering of ourselves and is actually not in integrity to the other person either, who must eventually help themselves if they are to address the problem.

As you can imagine, the fact that we can absorb others' energies poses some difficult questions. What are we supposed to do when we are ill? Should we treat the disease or "give it back" to someone else, much as I did with my familial allergies? If we sense another person in distress, do we even want to help them or are we going to end up with their issues as they end up without them? These are some of the concerns visited upon the sympathetic person, which can be encapsulated in the word "enmeshment," the state of being entangled so completely that it's hard to tell where you end and someone or something else begins.

Personalizing

When we are personalizing a situation, a process that therapists often call personal distress or personalizing instead of empathizing, we aren't experiencing the other's issues at all. Rather than sensing their direct experience, we are feeling only our own feelings, needs, issues, and reactions. However, we believe we are relating to the others' reality, although in fact we are using their pain as an excuse to dredge up our own or are using their situation as an excuse to talk about a similar one we have gone through. Of course, empathy often involves sharing our own experiences as a way to calm or soothe another. Personalization is a problem when the main reason we are "empathizing" is to put the focus on ourself, thus ignoring the other.

We might still hug the other person. We might still conjure up feelings of care or understanding for others or a situation. But we cannot truly understand what the other person is going through, nor will the other person believe that we really "get" them.

I have frequently experienced this situation. I have watched a narcissist sob as I talked about the death of a loved one, but I never had the sense that the person felt or "got" me. Rather, I felt like they were using my personal pain as a way to hook into their own reservoir of distress. I also sensed that they were acting in such a way as to either impress me or grab all the attention for themselves.

Sometimes we find ourselves personalizing another's pain and get overwhelmed by our own similar experience. I remember once listening to a friend's sorrow; she had just miscarried. I started crying, but not really out of concern for her. My friend's miscarriage stimulated my grief at having miscarried months before. I consciously pretended that my concern was for her but spend time later dealing with my own previously hidden grief. Next time I saw her, I was able to be present for my friend's pain. I didn't "use" it for my own emotional processing. Looking back, I wish I had simply told her that her story struck close to home and that I could be a better friend if I called her later, after I cleared my own undealt-with emotions.

Imagination

Some people confuse imagination with compassionate empathy, usually because they want to care but simply cannot. While we can perform make-believe empathic behaviors such as crying with someone, sighing at their pain, or laughing along in celebration, there is a hollow tone to conceptualized empathy. Of course, imagining what someone else is going through can help us eventually relate to them. If we cannot get to a point of truly relating, however, we risk our integrity. We lead the other on. They might start to think we understand and expect that our actions will be supportive, and then wonder why we continue on as if nothing had ever happened.

I once worked with a couple who were on the brink of divorce. She insisted that he wasn't empathic, even though he appeared to be kind and considerate. He nodded his head when she was sharing, and he leaned forward, holding her hand, when she was upset. The wife insisted, however, that his care wasn't genuine.

Finally the husband admitted that he had no idea about his wife's emotions. "I grew up in a house where feelings weren't allowed," he shared. "I guess I've learned how to play the part."

The husband's behavior worked for him in shallow relationships, such as at work or the health club. In his everyday world, everyone believed him to be compassionate and caring. But his wife could feel that he wasn't able to bond with her. The husband needed to do deep work in therapy if he was to unlock his own emotions, for without these, he wouldn't be able to relate empathically.

Pity

Pity is another substitute for empathy. When we pity someone, we feel sorry for them (and this can apply to ourselves as well). This stance automatically places us in a hierarchical, top-down position and disempowers the other person (or the part of ourselves that is in need of empathy). It can also cost us real energy.

Think about the last time someone pitied you, sending you cringe-worthy "poor you" vibes. Rather than feeling cared about, you probably felt even worse about the problem you were experiencing, as well as inadequate to address it. While we aren't responsible for everything that happens to us, we'll never recover from a trauma if we remain lost in the shadows of "poor me." We'll act like a victim and, at the same time, establish a cycle of entitlement in which we believe that because we are being victimized, others owe us.

I once worked with a woman who had been sexually abused while growing up. This is a horrifying situation, and I felt deep compassion for her. A few months into our work, however, I started to notice that her stories of abuse got wilder and wilder. In fact, outside of a Hollywood screenplay, they simply weren't physically possible. While I could empathize with the events that had a ring of truth, I couldn't connect with those that seemed so far out.

Finally she yelled at me, incensed that I wasn't providing her with enough pity. "You and the rest of the world *owe* me for what I've gone through!" she screamed.

Years later, she admitted that she embellished her memories with all her therapists and friends in order to get attention. She cared more about having people feel sorry for her than revealing her real problems. Basing their interactions on false information, her surrounding caregivers couldn't give her what she really needed. In fact, she was treated like a little girl instead of a functioning adult who could improve her own life. After trying for so many years, her life conditions went downward, not upward. Pity obscures the true needs and prevents the healing effects of empathy.

The other potential disaster area involved in pity is that when pitying another, we can easily end up carrying their energy. While we're sending care to someone who is in a pitiful state, it's easy for them to take advantage of our "poor you" attitude. They will simply agree to our unspoken offer and send us their problems.

Energy is energy. When we send another person compassion, we are sending pure love. The other can choose to accept or reject it, but the compassion doesn't return to us. It is an energy that keeps on giving at no cost to us unless we also choose to follow up with action. Pity, on the other hand, has a hook. Think of it as a beam of light with a hook at the end holding a bucket. This light strand plunges through another's energy field and body, and if the person really doesn't want to deal with their issues, they fill the bucket with themselves. When the light beam retracts, can you guess where that sludge gets dumped? (Feel it inside you yet?) It's important to ask ourselves if we really want to be potentially "gifted" with another's problems, as we can't fix a problem that is not our own. While we can support others as they care for themselves, we can't do it for them.

Emotional Contagion

Empathy is not sympathy, imagination, or pity. Neither is it emotional contagion. Sometimes we find ourselves getting caught up in an emotional frenzy. Everyone in a crowd is crying or laughing or having an out-of-body religious experience, and so are we.

These enflamed emotions only go so deep and are part of what I call group consciousness. A group of people can share emotions. Recently I worked with a young girl who attended a school that had lost three young people in a car accident. This girl, who hadn't known her three peers, felt the grief so deeply that she hadn't been able to eat or sleep for weeks. Her mother was puzzled when she learned this behavior was occurring throughout the school. While the mom empathized with her daughter's emotional struggles, as well as those the other kids were experiencing, she sensed they had gone too far.

The daughter was literally enmeshed in a group energy that promoted grief and misery. After I helped her unhook from this using some of the tools I offer in part II, I encouraged her to sense her actual feelings. The girl felt sad but not miserable. She went home that night and began to eat and sleep again.

Hyperoptimism

Another area I want to address is optimism, especially being hyper- or overoptimistic, the state that promotes mania or a seemingly blissed-out disassociation. Many people expect that empaths are more optimistic or happy than the less empathic, but this is not true. According to studies, emotional empathy does not necessarily lead to agreeableness, tranquility, or optimism. It is, plain and simple, the ability to relate to others when examined only from a human-to-human perspective.[36] To confuse empathy with the more ecstatic emotional states can create a distorted point of view about the true nature of empathy and of what we are supposed to act like when we are being empathic.

For instance, we might meet a highly energetic or gregarious individual and assume that they are empathic, only to discover that they lack a shred of understanding or compassion. While they may be relentlessly upbeat and hence seem capable of the kind of support a genuinely empathetic person can offer, they may, in fact, have great difficulty making meaningful contact; the outgoing personality can serve as a protective shield that actually precludes the ability to feel what another feels.

There are a variety of reasons for the shielding often involved in hyper-optimism. The over-optimistic/low empath might actually be overly sensitive. That armor might be the only way they think (unconsciously) they can separate from others and not dissolve into an emotional puddle. As well, their parents might have been very appearance oriented, modeling the belief that emotional safety or personal preservation is dependent on maintaining a sense of separation. No matter the reason, this cut-off coping mechanism leads to loneliness and isolation.

Sometimes people really think that if they act happy they can make a sad person feel better. They might feel uncomfortable with another's pain and try to alleviate it—for themselves. Or they might actually be empathizing but not know what to do; in their nervousness, they act a little goofy. Yet other hyperoptimistic individuals might be manipulating in order to be liked or to get what they want. They also may be in the manic state of a syndrome such as bipolar disorder, and this brings us to our last category.

Mental Maladjustment

Like the topic of sympathy, this last item on our list is important enough to discuss in depth, so I have added a section on mental maladjustment in the form of appendix 2. For now, it is sufficient to consider that certain people are incapable of empathy, while others use the empathic process in a maladjusted or manipulative way in order to meet their own needs.

For instance, I once had a friend who was enormously emotional and seemingly caring. He encouraged me to call him anytime I had a problem, and for quite some time, I did. It took me a couple of years (I'm slow), but eventually I noticed that the conversations that started with him emotionally "getting" me ended with him pouring his heart out to me and me agreeing to do him a favor. Once alerted, I started to watch his behavior with our mutual friends. Sure enough, this man's genuine empathic gift had warped into a disturbing ability to get others to hear his problems and deliver favors for him.

EMPATHIC EXPLORATION 3   *What Isn't Empathy?*

While reading through this chapter, you may have related to certain qualities that seemed like empathy but were not. As you answer the following questions, reflect upon any that you respond to with a yes, then see if you can figure out which of the seven types of empathic disguises they might be. Note that some of the questions relate to experiences within you. Other questions describe what you might have gone through with others. The correct labels for these experiences are listed after the exploration.

1. Have you ever felt like you couldn't tell the difference between your own feelings and someone else's?

2. Have you ever felt like you were drained of your own emotions or needs—like someone else had literally taken them on?

3. Have you ever had an emotional reaction to someone else's tragedy but felt like you were relating to your own trauma, not the other's situation?

4. Did you ever sense that someone's empathic reaction to you was hollow—like they were using your hardship or joyous expression to relive their own circumstances?

5. Did you ever walk away from an interaction with someone feeling like you had just faked your response?

6. Have you shared a success or challenge with someone and had the sense that though their empathic reaction appeared correct, it left you empty and disconnected from them?

7. Have you felt so sorry for someone going through a hard time that you felt compelled to fix everything for them?

8. Have you ever sensed that someone was so over-the-top in their desire to help you cope with an issue that they "took over"?

9. Have you had the experience of being so swept away in someone else's enthusiasm that you couldn't sense your own inner reality?

10. Were you ever part of a large group of people who were so devoted to a cause that you couldn't separate from their intensity and analyze what was really going on?

11. Are you aware of any times you've forced yourself to be "up" just to keep others afloat?

12. Have you ever spent time with someone who is so gregarious you can't help but wonder if they are being real or not? (You suspect they are not.)

13. Did you ever sense that you only related to someone else's life situation to get attention for your own?

14. Have you ever had a crazy-making feeling when someone else has appeared to be empathetic, caring, and giving only to make you do something for them?

Debriefing Your Empathic Exploration

Following are the types of empathy disguises that correspond to the questions you have just considered:

- Question 1: Sympathy/enmeshment
- Question 2: Sympathy/enmeshment
- Question 3: Personalizing
- Question 4: Personalizing
- Question 5: Imagination
- Question 6: Imagination
- Question 7: Pity
- Question 8: Pity
- Question 9: Emotional contagion

- Question 10: Emotional contagion
- Question 11: Hyperoptimism
- Question 12: Hyperoptimism
- Question 13: Mental maladjustment
- Question 14: Mental maladjustment

Truth be told, the empathic gifts are plentiful among the intuitive abilities. In order to safely and wisely develop your own gifts, assure that you don't misuse them, and respond intelligently to people who might be misusing their own, you must know what types of empathic gifts you have, which is the focus of the next chapter.

CHAPTER 4

Learn Your Type: The Six Empathic Styles

Our bodies have five senses: touch, smell, taste, sight, hearing. But not to be overlooked are the senses of our souls: intuition, peace, foresight, trust, empathy. The differences between people lie in their use of these senses; most people don't know anything about the inner senses while a few people rely on them just as they rely on their physical senses, and in fact probably even more.

C. JOYBELL C.

The first key to developing your empathic gifts is to know which ones you have. As I said at the outset, many of us believe there is but one empathic gift—called empathy—but this isn't true. There is an array of empathic gifts, and each one is as beautiful and rich as a great Impressionist painting.

The following story of two clients will help illustrate the diversity of the empathic world.

Like Father, Like Daughter?
Empathic Styles Collide

Connor, the father, and Jessica, age twelve, sat before me in my office. This father-daughter duo had made an appointment because they were struggling. The most important person in their combined world, Isabelle, had died a couple of years earlier: Connor's wife and Jessica's mother. Their common bond of grief was causing a ripple in their relationship, and in a most extraordinary way.

Since her mother had died, Jessica had started *feeling* spirits. She called them "wisps," as that's how they felt when they slid across her skin. She insisted that while most of the wisps were "from the house and the olden days," one of them was her mother.

The family lived in a stately old mansion in the South that had been around since before the Civil War. Having been occupied by many ancestors, it had seen considerable loss and death. Perhaps a dozen generations had passed through the house, leaving behind energetic representatives of the various families.

Jessica couldn't intuitively see these spirits, which would have marked her as clairvoyant. Nor could she hear them, which is a clairaudient trait. Rather, she felt what they felt and sensed what the most painful parts of their lives had entailed. She described a man with a stump leg who was in pain from a gunshot wound and the loss of his limb. In her own body, Jessica felt both his physical pain and his emotional reactions to his trauma. She also described a child who walked around the house, mournfully looking for his mother. The child-ghost believed that his mother had died when the opposite was actually true: the child had died and now could not find his mother, who had remained on the earthly plane.

Jessica also relayed stories of her mother, whom she believed showed up whenever a particularly songful robin perched in a bush outside her bedroom window. As soon as the bird started to sing, Jessica sensed the comforting presence of her mother, providing reassurance that she was still watching over both her and her father.

Connor was as empathic as his daughter but exhibited different forms of empathy. A medical doctor, he sensed others' physical distress in his own body. He almost always knew exactly where a patient hurt, although he seldom let on—he didn't want his patients to think he was weird. On one occasion he had found himself inwardly protesting a session with a patient who came in complaining of low-back pain. Because Connor actually began to feel an acute pain in his chest, however, he ordered an angiogram and determined that his patient was days away from a heart attack.

While Connor's sensitivity clearly assisted him on the job and benefited his clients, it also caused a rift between him and Jessica. Quite simply, Connor was so empathic that he couldn't stand the thought of leaving a patient in distress. He put in long hours, and in his limited free time he took shifts in the emergency room. He had vowed to be a doctor and saw no time clock associated with that promise. As long as people were in pain, he wasn't going to sit back and do nothing.

Whereas Jessica was highly attuned to the supernatural world, including the physical and emotional concerns of those in the afterlife, Connor was sensitive to the physical sensations of the living. One would imagine that the two would be able to relate. After all, weren't they both empathic? But that wasn't the case.

They were fighting because Jessica insisted that her father spend more time with her. From Connor's perspective, Jessica should stop "daydreaming" and start paying more attention to her school life. In fact, he was scared that she was actually emotionally immature. Connor believed that if Jessica would stop telling stories and simply make more friends, she would be less dependent on him.

Some of their problems certainly weren't unique. Connor was losing himself in his job, and Jessica wanted to hang on to her mother rather than venture into the world and potentially be hurt by life. I encouraged the two of them to work with a therapist in relation to these life issues, although we also discussed them to some extent. The extrasensory problems, however, were such that I felt competent to address them.

I pointed out to Connor that grief might have blasted open an innate empathic gift in his daughter, one that I call shamanic empathy. While she exhibited both emotional and physical empathy, which I'll describe in this chapter, she was clearly sensitive to mystical phenomena as well—the mark of a good shaman. Maybe, I told Connor, Isabelle—and other spirits—really were visiting Jessica, in which case he might want to both believe her and help her strategize a plan so she wouldn't be so vulnerable to their whims.

Connor was shocked (and not altogether pleased) when I suggested that he might be able to relate to Jessica as he, too, displayed a spiritual or intuitive gift.

"You mean I'm *psychic?*" he cried out, as if using a bad word.

I said, "Yes, although I prefer to use the word *empathic.*"

Connor had never considered his ability to sense another's physical discomfort as an intuitive gift. He was both pleased by this and afraid that his ability might be tainted with an otherworldly scent.

After I explained that his physical empathic gift was actually that—an innate way of being empathic, a kind of visceral intuition—he felt better. Although his ability was a great spiritual gift, I further explained, and one supportive of his spiritual mission and purpose, he didn't need to let it get the better of him. He could use it at work, but he didn't need to let it make him work all the time.

"Your daughter needs you," I said. "A spiritual gift makes room for all aspects of our life, not only the professional arena."

Over a couple of sessions, I taught Jessica how to modulate her gift (techniques you will also learn in part II) so she could be a "regular kid" and not always vulnerable to missives from the deceased. I also showed Connor ways he could stop the flow of information that caused him to pick up on everyone else's physical distress so that he, too, could lead a normal life—one that provided him ample time for fathering. And I invited both of them to embrace the spirit of Isabelle in such a way that she could continue her journey into the afterlife.

I have shared this particular story to showcase two of the many types of empathy. As you can see, both father and daughter were naturally gifted, but neither of them knew they were empathic. As a result, they hadn't developed their gifts appropriately.

As you read through the following outline and explanation of the basic empathic gifts, pay attention to which ones best describe you and your empathic experiences. After exploring these gifts, you'll be able to take a quiz that can further help you identify and define your empathic style.

The Six Empathic Styles

Nearly anyone can cultivate empathy. If you want to truly expand your empathic abilities to their compassionate best, you must first figure out which style is your strongest and begin there.

Of course, you don't need to concentrate solely on your strengths. You can always develop a weaker empathic style or even work on one that has yet to spring forth from your inner jack-in-the-box. It will be easier, however, to magnify those you are already partial to.

The following short descriptions will help you begin to get acquainted with the six empathic styles.

Physical

A physical empath absorbs physical energies present in the external environment. They can feel in their body the illness and pain in another's body. They might also be able to sense the physical energy held in an object. For instance, a physical empath can hold a piece of jewelry someone else has worn frequently and, in doing so, sense the physical aches, pains, and pleasures of that other person inside themselves. Physical empaths might also embody one or more of the clair gifts associated with empathy I mentioned earlier, including clairgustance (clear tasting), clairscent (clear smelling), and clairtangency (clear touching). How might these various subaspects of physical empathy weave together? As an example, a full-blown physical empath with access to all these gifts might sense another's bodily aches and pains, the taste in the other's mouth, the smell of their perfume or aftershave, and the feeling of clothing on their skin.

Emotional

An emotional empath feels another's feelings as if they are their own. This also is called clairempathy (clear feeling) by some psychics and clairsentience (clear sensing) by others, terms presented in the introduction. As I mentioned there, I usually avoid these terms, finding "emotional empathy" more straightforward.

Mental

The mental empath receives information and data from the outside world and seems to simply "know" what someone else knows. This style may involve clairsentience and claircognizance (clear knowing) as well as clairaudience (clear hearing) and clairvoyance (clear seeing).

Natural

The natural empath relates to nature-based forces and creatures. Through this capacity the empath can tap into far-flung environmental sources of information, including such wonders as planetary shifts and weather patterns, the emotions and needs of animals, and ways in which an herb can be used for healing purposes. A wide array of psychic gifts can factor into natural empathy: clairgustance, clairscent, clairtangency, clairempathy (clear feeling), clairsentience, and claircognizance.

Spiritual

Spiritual empaths sense the heart of the Divine and often are able to determine what "God wants" (or does not want) for themselves or others. They're also especially adept at intuitively feeling another person's level of honesty or dishonesty. Here, the gifts of clairsentience and claircognizance are key.

Shamanic

I use the term *shamanic* to describe the sixth empathic type because I have observed that there are certain extradimensional empathic abilities as well. I experience these myself, and this is the category of empath I fit into. In terms of the clairs, all of the empathic gifts are available to the shamanic empath to one degree or another.

The ancient practice of shamanism has appeared in a variety of forms around the world and through time, but a connecting thread is that the shaman perceives spirit everywhere and in everything. Another common element is that shamans are able to tune in to extra dimensions: other-worldly beings as well as other times, places, and spaces. With this capacity and the ability to work with all the other forms of empathy I have just briefly described, the shamanic empath possesses a multidimensional awareness that can include an awareness of others' past lives, the sense of spiritual presences, or knowledge about what might have occurred in a house or on a specific piece of land. This awareness can involve psychic navigation, or drawing on a variety of signals offered by the other empathic gifts, and it is marked by a knowing of what someone needs in order to make an effective life decision or invite healing. As we will see with the other styles of empathy, the shamanic empath is also a frequent conveyor of what might occur in the future through a process I call radiant empathy, which we will discuss a little further on. Basically, the shaman empath can do it all—which, I can attest, can feel like both a great gift and an overwhelming curse.

As we now explore these six basic types of empathic spiritual gifts more completely, give yourself permission to wander the annals of your memory banks. Have you had any of the experiences noted for each category? Do you know others who have shared—or complained of—these abilities? Empathy becomes real when we see it demonstrated by others or ourselves; it makes a difference in our own or others' lives when we ignore the temptation to be merely sympathetic, such as to only pity another or be artificially optimistic, and retain our own identity even while sensing another's reality.

Physical Empathy:
Two Bodies as One

Have you ever stood next to a person with a physical malady, pain, or illness, only to find yourself mimicking their discomfort, down to feeling each and every ache and pain? Or maybe you've been near someone who is in tip-top condition and you, consequently, feel as healthy as Atlas, the Greek Titan who is strong enough to hold up the world. This is the basic indication of physical empathy: the capacity for sensing another's physicality in your own body. Added to the ability to mirror others' physical sensations is the capacity to attune to physical objects such as those near and dear to a living being.

For example, I have a friend who is so physically empathic that she can't buy jewelry or clothing from a consignment store. She has only to touch or put on the item and she senses what the previous owner used to feel like physically. She once bought an old-fashioned cameo necklace but couldn't wear it because she felt like she had arthritis in her joints when she had it on. Another time she purchased a pair of pants and sensed bruising all over her legs.

In these two cases, she eventually asked the storekeeper about the items' previous owners. The storekeeper refused to name names but did confirm that the cameo owner was an older woman with arthritis and that the pants had been consigned by a woman undergoing chemotherapy for leukemia. One of the side effects of leukemia is bruising.

On the plus side, imagine the benefits of being a physical empath if you are a doctor, nurse, or other type of healer who can attune to a patient and run the correct tests. Physical empathy gives moms and dads an advantage, too, as they are able to sense when something might be amiss with their children. The compassionate physical empath can creatively assist individuals with refraining from deleterious behaviors or actions, or recovering from physical maladies that have already cropped up. And they can readily figure out what kinds of activities or situations are healthy and supportive for them.

As well, many physical empaths develop their gifts so they can actually program or shift physical matter. They might hold a crystal in their hands and send healing energy into it, which can then infuse the ill with assistance. They might sense a pain in a friend and then feel or conjure what relief would like, thereby "wishing" this into their friend. I explore these types of empathic behaviors in the section "Empathy By Transmission: Radiant Empathy and the Six Empathic Styles" later in this chapter.

On the other hand, physical empaths might find themselves stricken with the very same pains, diseases, and irksome problems as the people around them. This is a sure sign of being physically sympathetic instead of empathetic. Sure, they might sense another's head cold, but do they really want to end up suffering from it? Along these same lines, some physical empaths are so sensitive to others' objects that, like my friend, they refrain from touching things other people have owned.

Physical empaths must make sure they know the difference between their own material sensations and those of others. As well, they might need to figure out if they hold unconscious beliefs that cause them to take a backseat to another's predicament. Questions to ask include "Do I believe my physical well-being is less important than another's? Do I think my ultimate value is to serve others, even to my own detriment?"

It can then be helpful to cultivate an response to physical sympathy. For instance, when I sense another's physical distress, I ask the Divine, "How am I to be with this?" I ask my own essential self to return energy not suitable for me or to give me insight or a sign of how I'm to help another without cost to myself. Be reinstating myself into the picture, I shift from a sympathetic to an empathetic state.

Emotional Empathy:
An Abundance of Feelings

To emotional empaths, the world is like a Crayola kaleidoscope of feelings. They may find themselves oohing and aahing at the treasure trove of feelings emanating from others, which are almost too numerous to count.

Actually, there are only five basic families of feelings: happiness, sadness, fear, anger, and disgust. To these, many experts are now adding the category of pain, and others add contempt and surprise, while yet other experts substitute joy and surprise for happiness. Within these several areas, however, are thousands of secondary feelings, all of which every human being (and maybe even other life forms) cycle through on a regular, if not sometimes moment-to-moment, basis. Aspects of happiness include contentment, gratitude, bliss, calm, and satisfaction. Open the box of anger and you will find frustration, irritation, rage, and more.

The most gifted emotional empaths are often described as being "highly sensitive," a trait that can be overwhelming but also beneficial. According to several observers—including John D. Mayer of the University of New Hampshire, who, along with Peter Salovey from Yale University, wrote a breakthrough paper in 1990 titled *Emotional Intelligence*—people with emotional intelligence, or EI, are able to reason about emotions and use feelings to enhance higher thinking. For instance, people who can relate to others' sadness show higher analytical skills than people who cannot. People with emotional intelligence can better manage their own and others' emotions and connect their own broad array of sensitivities to recognize them in others.[37] They are more likely to have a better social support system and fewer problematic interactions with others, such as fights and interpersonal violence. They are also less likely to use drugs and alcohol.[38]

There is a dark side to emotional empathy. An abusive environment can warp a person's innate emotional empathy. In order to "self-protect" or survive, the emotional empath might end up tuning in to others' emotions in order to manipulate them. They can learn to use their tone of voice to silence or scare others, use their own words against them, or convince them of lies. A distorted emotional empath will tend to tell someone what they want to hear in order to get their own needs met.

Emotional empaths are also famous for being personally sensitive and having their own feelings easily hurt. As a consequence, they can become threatening as another way to self-protect. Their defensiveness is an avoidance of further pain, which can potentially make them bitter, cynical, and verbally abusive. They can also lay excellent guilt trips but turn around and apologize when it serves them—another form of manipulation if the apology is not heart-centered.[39]

Yet another challenge for many emotional empaths is the difficulty in separating their own emotions from those of others. I have had thousands of clients call me to ask, "Is this my emotion or someone else's? Do I like this job or am I feeling others' attraction to this job? Do I love my partner or am I simply feeling their feelings for me?"

This form of emotional sympathy can lead to illness. I once worked with a woman who was overly bonded to her mother when she was growing up. By the time the daughter was thirty years old, the mother had several autoimmune diseases, including diverticulitis and chronic fatigue syndrome. Her daughter displayed many of the same maladies, although there isn't a direct genetic correlation in health issues like chronic fatigue. These physical diseases, however, are often linked to emotional problems, which is one of the reasons I was certain that the daughter had spent her life absorbing her mother's emotions, sacrificing herself in the process. After helping the daughter decide that she didn't need to take in her mother's emotions—that a greater force or God could help her mother instead—her autoimmune symptoms all but disappeared. The mother hit bottom and went into therapy, where she began dealing with her own emotional challenges.

Mental Empathy:
Data, Data Everywhere

There are some people who simply seem to know everything and anything, even though they swear they haven't swallowed the *Encyclopedia Britannica*. In modern parlance, these are our walking and talking Wikipedias. If you are one of these individuals, you might very well be a mental empath, someone who relates to information and data from the outside world.

One of my best friends is a mental empath. I seldom research a project without first running my ideas by him. I might present my theories to him, such as, "I think that cancer is always caused by a virus," and he might say, "My sense is that you need to investigate morphing or transforming microbes."

Has he ever read a medical textbook? Nope.

Certain mental empaths specialize in different areas of expertise. One might access information about other people's personal lives, such as insights about their beliefs, fears, or deep desires. Other empaths might understand financial numbers, agricultural anomalies, or the best way to manage a project. Still others focus on data about anything from coins to angels. At the core of all mental empathic abilities, however, is access to information and perceptions.

Mental empathy can be a challenging gift. It raises the question of "how do I know what I know?" Essentially, empathy is a body-based intuitive process and one that only can be proven by its effectiveness. The only way to substantiate the empathic awareness of information is to wait and see if it's accurate. This cause-and-effect gap can leave empaths questioning their abilities. It can also leave them feeling defensive or ill-prepared when others ask to prove or substantiate their claims.

I once worked with a youngster who had an excellent sense of mental empathy, so much so that she aced almost every exam she ever took, except, for some odd reason, in social studies. Her teachers accused her of cheating and so did her parents, because she hardly ever cracked a book and she nodded off during many classes. Her mental empathy resulted in scholastic brilliance. Based on my advice, she learned to at least pretend to listen and study, just to get people off her back while she was going through school.

There are many other facets of mental empathy, two of which we can see through the eyes of Daniel Goleman, well-known author of *Emotional Intelligence*. According to Goleman, cognitive empathy encompasses the following activities:

- understanding how others think about things
- the ability to take another's perspective[40]

When we relate to another's thoughts, we can better understand how they see the world and, therefore, why they do what they do. Sometimes we might feel the need to intervene—to provide additional data so the person can make a better choice. For instance, I once worked with a client who refused to leave her alcoholic husband. My own mental empathy style helped me understand that she thought of herself as worthless. After I helped her correct this misperception, she was eventually able to leave her husband because she was able to change her belief system from a self-negating one to a self-loving one. And in the process of working with her, I was able to "upgrade" my mental empathy to the stage of compassion, which enabled me to actually make a difference.

At the core, mental empathy invites us to step into someone else's perspective, and not only in present-day time. I once worked with a mental empath who was a historical scholar. He could literally sense the thought structures and perspectives of long-dead figures in history. He was able to interweave his intuitive perspectives into the textbooks he wrote, garnering kudos from critics, who found his insights eerily observant.

The upside of mental empathy, when utilized with compassion, is as I shared earlier: if you can enter another's mental world, you can understand them and, if necessary, help them shift from a negative perception to a more life-affirming one. You can provide motivation and education and promote transformational change. On the downside, mental empaths might also be tempted to apply their perceptions to manipulating or controlling others. To know can be a great thing if the knowledge is lovingly offered.

Natural Empathy:
From the Sinewy Serpents
to the Sparkling Stars

Have you ever heard of a horse whisperer? These special individuals practice something called "natural horsemanship." They relate so well to the horse that they don't need to use violent or pain-inducing means of training. And there are a number of other kinds of whisperers, including people who naturally relate with dogs, birds, sharks, wolves, lions, and even bears.[41] These individuals are all part of the empathic group I call the natural empaths.

Many professional whisperers attribute their ability to an innate understanding of the animals they work with, as well as strong observational and disciplinary skills. But some people who are sensitive to animals come right out and say it: they are psychically empathic, able to attune to and communicate with beings in the natural world. When empathy extends to beings and forces in nature, it is called natural empathy.

A natural empath is able to attune to aspects of nature, both animate and inanimate. Some natural empaths are sensitive to almost anything in nature, including animals, reptiles, birds, plants, trees, and rocks. They may also be tuned in to the moon, planets, stars, and elements, such as water, earth, fire, and air. Basically, a natural empath could conceivably sense what is occurring in any part of the natural world.

Some natural empaths are more attuned to one form of nature than any other. For example, a natural empath might relate primarily to animals and, within this group, only dogs. In fact, they might be somewhat of a niche empath, only empathizing with dachshunds or golden retrievers. The same works for all other categories of nature, from serpents to stars. Natural sensitives might perform any of the other five forms of empathy (or a combination of them) but would consider themselves natural empaths if the gift is applied solely to beings, objects, or forces of nature.

Some people can attune to human beings *and* beings of nature, however, in which case they might acquire a long list of empathic types after their names. For instance, I once worked with a man who could sense everyone else's feelings—and I mean everyone's. It didn't matter if the subject was nearby or on the other side of the world; he always knew what the object of his focus felt. He could also sense what animals were feeling emotionally. He was especially attuned to dogs, probably because he was raised with them as a child and loved them. I would label this client both an emotional and natural empath.

Still other natural empaths are inclusive of or exclusive to other aspects of nature, such as plants or lakes, stars or the wind. I once worked with a shaman from Peru who could attune to all the area's healing plants. He grew them in his garden. When I was in his presence, I could touch one of these plants and figure out what healing properties it bestowed. I cannot perform this task in America, which makes me wonder if I "borrowed" this shaman's natural empathy through my own shamanic empathy, which we will explore later in this chapter.

I have met individuals with as many different forms of natural empathy as could be conceived of. I once taught a class on empathy for which close to fifty people showed up. One woman was an astrologer who could mentally "read" both her clients and what the planets were up to. She was, therefore, both a mental and natural empath. Another woman related to whales. She could sense what very particular whales were going through thousands of miles away. She was a clear natural empath. Yet another man made his living as a jeweler, but his real gift wasn't as commonplace as his job title lets on. He could actually sense information and feelings in rocks.

And another class attendant used rocks for healing purposes. She was able to hold a rock and figure out what it could do for a person's physical ailment or life issue.

Many natural empaths draw on the same information as do emotional, mental, physical, and spiritual empaths, especially when working with nature's creatures, such as fish, fowl, animals, or birds. They can sense a dog's physical aches and pains, feel its feelings, relate to its perceptions, and figure out what the Divine would like (or not) for this very important being.

When natural empathy is used wisely and appropriately, the empath is able to relate to beings and forces that are seldom represented on this planet. They can assist others in taking care of their pets, tending their gardens, or connecting to nature in general. Other natural empaths can access the natural world to assist people or animals that need healing or tending to. Still others, such as those who are able to read the stars and natural forces, can help people navigate decision making or prepare for a storm.

The compassionate natural empath makes sure that there is no harm done to either nature or people and that the human and natural world are allowed to live in balance and harmony.

Some natural empaths are so influenced by energetic information that they can become overwhelmed by the pain, suffering, or needs of nature. I once worked with a client who couldn't drive along most major highways because she could sense the grief of standing trees that had lost their neighboring trees to logging or pruning. I have another client who can't hike in the mountains if there has been strip mining nearby because she can feel the cutting of the rocks in her own bones.

Of course, there are also those natural empaths who misuse their gift. The proverbial story is of the mentally imbalanced teenager who tortures or kills animals. The pain and suffering inflicted on an animal most likely mirrors their own, and by projecting it onto an animal, they can somehow gain a sense of mastery over their own victimization issues. By and large, however, I have found that natural empaths are sweet and sensitive souls, here to create harmony between nature and humanity. One of my friends is such a high natural empath that she has adopted three dogs and ten cats from the Animal Humane Society and teaches others how to rescue animals.

Everything in nature gives off a vibration, and it is to this that a natural empath attunes. All is alive with vibration and voice, scent and sight, as John Muir captured so beautifully:

> *A few minutes ago every tree was excited, bowing to the roaring storm, waving, swirling, tossing their branches in glorious enthusiasm like worship. But though to the outer ear these trees are now silent, their songs never cease. Every hidden cell is throbbing with music and life, every fiber thrilling like harp strings, while incense is ever flowing from the balsam bells and leaves.*[42]

To the natural empath, the entirety of the world is alive—not only shimmering with life, but also breathing life into us.

Spiritual Empathy: Living in the Light

Every one of us is a spirit. We are an immortal and unique spark birthed from the flame of the Divine. Certain people, those whom I call spiritual empaths, are able to attune to others' spirits and also to the Greater Spirit's intentions and dreams.

To the spiritual empath, all of life is a prayer. It is an expression of divine blessing. A spiritual empath inherently knows that the purpose of life is to live as the blessings we are, primarily through service to others. If we could only live in this way, as the spiritual empath knows, there would be no war or violence, only peace and caring.

The spiritual empath is highly attuned to these higher and more universal goals as well as to individuals' personal goals. I'm not talking about career or relational goals—rather, the primary objectives that each of our spirits establishes for a lifetime. These aims are expansive and include the development of virtues, spiritual qualities, and ways of being that lead to what I call practical enlightenment, or the ability to express divinely through human endeavors.

A spiritual empath can sometimes feel or sound judgmental because they are able to discern the difference between how someone is currently living or expressing their purpose and how they are supposed to be acting. A spiritual empath often reads these differences in their own body or through an inexplicable but overwhelming awareness.

Here are a couple of scenarios that will better explain spiritual empathy.

Imagine that a spiritual empath is attending church and listening to a pastor. As the pastor preaches, the spiritual empath starts to feel uncomfortable, maybe a little hot under the collar or sick to his stomach. He looks around to see if anyone notices that he is alternatively sweating and getting chills. He has the vague sense that something is really off with the pastor's sermon, but no one else seems to notice. Instead, the audience is staring straight ahead, enraptured—except, of course, for that kid who is kicking the pew in front of him, bored to death.

The twisted feeling in the spiritual empath's stomach grows—and then he knows. The preacher isn't walking his own talk. Though he has no apparent way to prove this observation, the empath's body relaxes. At some level, he knows, the man behind the pulpit is out of integrity.

Here is another scenario.

Meet the female spiritual empath who is a therapist. She is sitting in her office, facing a couple. The husband is obviously struggling. His clothes are mismatched and rumpled and his beard is straggly. He looks like he's hardly able to function. In contrast, the woman is straitlaced and meticulously put together. The buttons on her suit coat gleam as if they were actually polished.

The wife is relaying that her husband is an alcoholic. The man's head hangs in shame as she discusses his exploits. The entire time the wife is talking, the spiritual empath feels dirty, like something is wrong or discolored with this woman.

The husband admits to his problem and says he wants to get help. The empathic therapist feels a warm and loving feeling toward the husband despite his life issues. No matter how hard she tries, however, the therapist can't feel good about the wife, even though the woman presents as near perfect.

Spiritual empaths don't read appearances alone; they are able to sense how genuine and honest someone is. An alcoholic who owns his issues is far more authentic and trustworthy than a well-mannered and accomplished person who doesn't own any of their dark, or shadow, side.

As you can imagine, the gift of being able to sense someone's spiritual integrity can be confusing, at least until you learn to recognize the internal signs that indicate who is straightforward, or "on-path," and who is not. Once a spiritual empath has learned to trust their internal recognition of honesty and ethics, they can help others recognize their own areas of spiritual weakness, as well as figure out what to do about them. Many spiritual empaths enter a form of ministry, life coaching, spiritual directing, or even business leadership—all paths that assist others in becoming all they can become.

The challenges are complex, however. No one likes to think poorly of others. A spiritual empath recognizes others' true potential but also understands the differences between potential and reality. It isn't easy, fun, or popular to acknowledge or point out the glaring discrepancies. Many spiritual empaths prefer to ignore their own gifts rather than face facts about other people, particularly family members or loved ones.

In the end, I believe the following passage from Michael Cobley's book *Seeds of Earth* best describes the compassionate outreach of a spiritual empath toward others:

> *"Dreams persist," the Pathmaster sighed. "The stronger the dreamer, the more resilient the dream. Some dream outward*

dreams, seeking unity with the external; others dream inwardly, dreams of hunger and conquest, of pain and the escape from pain. Some do not dream at all."[43]

The spiritual empath can intuitively read or sense another's dreams. Are they focused only on repeating the patterns and programs that have led to selfishness, spiritual starvation, or emptiness? Have they lost the ability to dream or to believe in anything at all or are they dreaming of the goodness implied in every atom, breath, and moment? The calling of the spiritual empath is to help everyone dream bigger and grander dreams for themselves and for all.

Shamanic Empathy: Every Facet of the Gem

Shamans are the priest-healers of their clans. Since the beginning of time, no matter whether a village was located in a desert, mountain, jungle, or even in the middle of a city, the shaman has been the appointed keeper of all things mystical, especially those things that return us to wholeness in body, mind, and soul.

While most people have one, two, or maybe even three empathic gifts, the shaman empath displays every empathic gift. A typical shamanic empathic interaction would be to sense what is occurring in another's body, feel their feelings, know what they are thinking, sense what is occurring in the natural world around them, figure out whether they are in spiritual accord with their actions or not, and—as if that's not enough—tune in to otherworldly phenomena as well.

A shaman might not access all of the other five types of empathy at the same time but is able to use any style when necessary. As I mentioned, I am a shaman empath, and because of this I have had to work on filtering out empathic data so that I'm not overloaded. For instance, I frequently attend my son's baseball games and often struggle with all kinds of sensations in that setting. I feel my son's joy when he gets on base, but also the disappointment of the other team's pitcher. I can tell which fellow parent is hungry and whether they have money for popcorn or not. (If not, I often pass my own bucket around.) I can tell if it's going to rain—or if we'll have snow, a tornado, or a sudden rise in temperature—and even figure out which attending pet is going to sit quietly by their owner's feet instead of chasing the balls that escape the park. I often remind myself to simply focus on the batter so I don't get overinvolved in clairs that keep me from enjoying the game.

I share this snippet to show how easy it is for a shaman empath to know *too* much. The shamanic experience is further complicated by the fact that shamans attune to more than the day-to-day events in others and the cosmos. If I really opened up during a baseball game, I'd probably be able to have a conversation with a youngster's deceased relatives! Shaman empaths have a proclivity for exposing themselves to beings and situations in other dimensions and time periods.

While the physical empath might touch an object and sense another's bodily issues, a shaman could touch the same object and inform you about that person's past lives, their pets, their health issues, and what the future might hold. While the spiritual shaman can sense another's spiritual destiny, determining whether they are on-path or not, the shaman can peer through the lens of time to see if that person's soul has ever been on the path toward that destiny, and, if so, during which life. As well, they might share information about one of the person's invisible spiritual guides—say, an angel or a deceased relative—while forewarning about a potential car accident.

For me, as well as for many shaman empaths I've worked with, the most challenging aspect of this empathic style involves distinguishing between past, present, and future; your body senses each of these time periods right now—in the present. It's also difficult to figure out whether what you are sensing applies to yourself or someone else.

For example, one night I lay in bed completely out of sorts. My chin hurt. I felt scared. I kept reviewing my car insurance policy. I had the sense of a dark presence. Was I remembering a car accident I'd had years earlier that I needed to revisit for some reason? Was I about to be struck down in the near future? Was I feeling an experience that a friend was currently suffering through?

I didn't get my answer until the next day. At precisely 2:00 PM, both my children had accidents. Michael was in a head-on car crash and Gabe was hurt at daycare, injuring his chin. Every sensation I had experienced the night before played out that day, down to my sense of Gabe's hurt chin and the need to call the car insurance company. I could only guess that remaining awake the night before had kept my adrenaline charged so I could take charge.

The compassionate shaman uses their multilayered experience to help the people and beings that the Divine asks them to assist. However, the wise shaman doesn't help everyone, even if asked for help. They don't feel everyone's feelings or move every toad that is in danger of being run over off the road. Rather, they learn how to rely on divine inspiration, sensing the empathic information that is presented through the filter of the Divine and abstaining from getting involved unless directed by the Divine.

The shaman empath who reports for duty to the Divine can be defined as a healer in the truest sense of the word: one who invites wholeness where there has been a perception of brokenness. The shaman empath is truly a doctor of the soul.

Empathy by Transmission: Radiant Empathy and the Six Empathic Styles

As an empath, you are usually in receiving mode. You are sensing, feeling, knowing, or relating to what is occurring inside another, whether the other is a person, another form of life, an object, or an energetic force. If you are committed to love and care, you might take the next step and act or think compassionately, appropriately seeking to alleviate another's suffering or support their evolution. There is another side to the empathy coin, however, that is seldom discussed or understood. I call it radiant empathy, and it is another means for serving others compassionately by using energetic rather than concrete means to provide assistance.

While empathy involves receiving energetic information, radiant empathy involves sending assistance energetically. It is a transmission process whereby the empath actually sends helpful and loving energy to another in order to relieve their pain and suffering or to offer insight and guidance.

Think of radiant empathy in terms of an email exchange. We all receive emails, maybe too many and too frequently. The empath is constantly opening emails that enable them to know what is occurring in the outside world. Many empaths are in danger of either closing off their abilities or becoming too sympathetic because they don't know that they don't have to physically respond to every email. They can become underempathic as a way of protecting themselves or overempathic and maybe overinvolved as a way of serving.

Radiant empathy offers another option. It involves responding to others' needs energetically rather than tangibly. In other words, you can answer an email instead of leaving your office, trekking to another's abode, and sitting in front of them. While the recipient of your compassionate response might not physically hear, see, or even sense your response, it can still be effective.

Any form of empathy can invite a radiant empathy response to another's needs. A physical empath might sense another's injury and send healing energy. A physical empath can bless an object for the ill, programming it so it emanates healing energy when the person sees, holds, or wears it.

Some physical empaths are so inclined toward radiant empathy that their gifts evolve into telekinesis, the ability to move objects without touching them. Sometimes trauma blasts open a physical empath's energetic field. Their strong reaction to their own condition can generate magnetic or electromagnetic fields that can literally move objects. Other physical empaths use their telekinesis ability to perform psychic surgery, energetically parting another's flesh so as to remove cysts, tumors, illnesses, or other conditions causing health problems. They might also sense the issues causing a physical disorder, such as emotional repression or poor posture. These healers can also insert healthy energy to affect transformation.

An emotional empath might sense another's sadness and send emotional assurance and love, kind of like a big teddy bear hug. A mental empath, on the other hand, might perceive that someone believes himself to be stupid and send back a corrective truth, affirming the other's intelligence and brilliance.

A natural empath can send healing energy to any being or force in nature but might also be able to direct a natural being or elemental force to help another person. For instance, one natural empath I know can send the vibrational qualities of rocks and plants into her clients so they can better heal. Another can call to her clients their power animals, which are the spirits of animals, reptiles, and birds willing to provide guidance.

A spiritual empath might pick up on someone's broken spirit and wish for them the power of grace, and a shamanic empath might do any of the above in addition to directing intrusive entities away from a person and asking for beneficial entities to show up and provide assistance.

This direct transference can occur without any in-person exchange, although I can also sit across from a client in my office and send radiant empathy. The point is that I do not need to be present to accomplish this goal. Such is the nature of radiant empathy.

EMPATHIC EXPLORATION 4 *What Is Your Style?*

We all have access to at least one empathic way of knowing, or style. Think about how you usually relate to people. Do you feel others' emotions in your own body, know what they know, or are you more prone to spiritual or mystical understandings?

To get a sense of which of the six empathic abilities might best describe you, I invite you to take the following test. Read each question and circle a number between 0 and 5, 0 meaning that the statement does not fit at all and 5 indicating a strong fit. You will assess and debrief the quiz when you are done.

1. I take on the physical pains of people around me.
   0 1 2 3 4 5

2. I am sensitive to the moods and feelings of others.
   0 1 2 3 4 5

3. I often understand what is motivating someone, even if they don't know understand themselves.
   0 1 2 3 4 5

4. I can often tell what animals are going through, physically or emotionally.
   0 1 2 3 4 5

5. I often feel the presence of nonphysical beings.
   0 1 2 3 4 5

6. I often feel like a stranger on this planet, like I'm so aware of other times and spaces that it's hard to tune in to the world around me.
   0 1 2 3 4 5

7. I often feel others' bodily symptoms of pain or illness in my own body.
   0 1 2 3 4 5

8. Strangers approach me and share their most deeply held feelings for no perceivable reason.
   0 1 2 3 4 5

9. I find it difficult to explain to people how I know what I know.

0 1 2 3 4 5

10. I often predict shifts in weather or environmental situations, even before they are announced.

0 1 2 3 4 5

11. I get a sense of inner peace around people who seem to live the values they proclaim.

0 1 2 3 4 5

12. I'm sometimes overwhelmed by my own psychic sensitivities to people, animals, objects, and even spirits. It's like I have all of the empathic gifts.

0 1 2 3 4 5

13. I can sometimes hold an object and experience strong sensations, such as the lightheadedness, nausea, or other sensations that the owner might have once experienced or may currently be experiencing.

0 1 2 3 4 5

14. I often feel a surge of emotion right before an event with a big outcome, regardless of whether it turns out to be really positive or negative.

0 1 2 3 4 5

15. It's easy for me to read between the lines and know what people are really thinking or saying.

0 1 2 3 4 5

16. I am happiest when in harmony with nature: earth, water, and skies.

0 1 2 3 4 5

17. I think we are all here fulfilling a divine destiny, and I like helping people figure out their own purpose.

0 1 2 3 4 5

18. Sometimes I'm more aware of the nonphysical worlds, dimensions, and beings than I am of the physical world.

0 1 2 3 4 5

19. I can feel the energy of the previous owners or visitors when I walk into a house.

0 1 2 3 4 5

20. I can usually tell if someone is in deep sorrow, even if they do not speak about it.

0 1 2 3 4 5

21. It's easy for me to get a sense of another's perspective, even if I don't know them well.

0 1 2 3 4 5

22. I have a natural green thumb, automatically knowing when to water plants or offer them more sunlight.

0 1 2 3 4 5

23. I can always tell when someone is lying or being dishonest.

0 1 2 3 4 5

24. I seem to have every sense of empathy: physical, emotional, mental, natural, and spiritual.

0 1 2 3 4 5

25. I often know exactly where in the body someone is injured or ill.

0 1 2 3 4 5

26. Sometimes I feel waves of strong emotions, only to later meet someone who is experiencing those feelings.

    0 1 2 3 4 5

27. I seem to know exactly what information to pay attention to, seemingly for no reason at all.

    0 1 2 3 4 5

28. Astrological or astronomical events often greatly affect or disturb me.

    0 1 2 3 4 5

29. Lack of ethics and integrity bothers me more than anything.

    0 1 2 3 4 5

30. I get déjà vu about others' pasts, including past lives.

    0 1 2 3 4 5

Debriefing Your Empathic Exploration: What Is Your Style?

Part I: Tallying the Questions

Please record your 0 to 5 scores for the questions related to the specific types of empathy. Then total the number of points you put in each of the six areas.

PHYSICAL EMPATHY

Question 1

Question 7

Question 13

Question 19

Question 25

> *Total physical empathy score:*

EMOTIONAL EMPATHY

Question 2

Question 8

Question 14

Question 20

Question 26

Total emotional empathy score:

MENTAL EMPATHY

Question 3

Question 9

Question 15

Question 21

Question 27

Total mental empathy score:

NATURAL EMPATHY

Question 4

Question 10

Question 16

Question 22

Question 28

Total natural empathy score:

SPIRITUAL EMPATHY

Question 5

Question 11

Question 17

Question 23

Question 29

Total spiritual empathy score:

Question 6

Question 12

Question 18

Question 24

Question 30

 Total shamanic empathy score:

 Total combined score:

Part II: Comparing Styles

As you have seen, you can potentially receive a total of 25 points for each of the six different empathic styles. The higher your points in a category, the higher your aptitude in that form of empathy. And the higher your total combined points, the greater your overall empathic potential or abilities.

You might have only one strong category or perhaps several areas of high empathy. People typically claim one or two forms of empathy as their own. Shamans, however, will most likely have high points in each category as well as in the shamanic area because, as we have seen, shamans usually display every form of empathy.

Following is a brief interpretation of the point totals that will help you determine whether your proficiency is high, medium, or low in regard to each of the six forms of empathy.

HIGH EMPATHY: *20 to 25 points*

You are highly empathic in this gift area. You often rely on this empathic style to relate to the outside world and would greatly benefit from learning how to set up appropriate boundaries so your experience does not overwhelm you. You might also want to practice ways of compassionately applying this empathic style to assist others, as you could be of great service when employing it with awareness and care.

MEDIUM EMPATHY: *12 to 19 points*

You show promise in this area of empathy. It has been useful for you and is a gift that most likely appears when others really need it. It would be worth your while to develop this style and learn how to use it when you feel like it can be beneficial to yourself and others.

LOW EMPATHY: *0 to 11 points*

This style is either not usable or accessible to you. It might be blocked due to simple lack of use or because of unresolved childhood or emotional issues. However, it could become available if you choose to examine any potential blockage and clear it. It is also possible that this empathic style is simply not "meant to be" for you, and it isn't necessary for you to employ or develop it.

TOTAL COMBINED SCORE

There is a potential of 125 total points. Certain individuals are strong in several categories, which is reflected in a higher total combined score, such as between 90 and 125 points. Others find their strengths in two main areas and might achieve a score of only 50 out of 125 points, which simply indicates that you have empathic strengths and weaknesses. The total combined score is mainly of interest if you score extremely high or low. A high score indicates a highly empathic nature—and the subsequent challenges, such as the need to distinguish your own energy from that of others and learn how to care for yourself. You might want to pay particular attention to developing your sense of self and energetic boundaries. A lower score, such as under 25 if the points are dispersed rather than contained in one or two categories, could suggest that you have blocked your empathy and might want to conduct some personal work to figure out why.

Good work! Now you have a clearer picture of how you operate as an empath. In order to further develop your empathic gifts, let's move on to part II for some practical application.

PART II

Application
Mastering the Gift of Empathy

Equipped with a new understanding of empathy along with a greater awareness of the integral role it can play in your daily life, you are now ready to apply it to the situations and moments that matter most to you. In part II you will learn practical techniques for activating compassionate empathy in matters such as physical and emotional healing, personal relationships, work, parenting, spiritual growth, and more. As you use the tools and tips offered in the pages ahead on a consistent basis, exciting changes will be afoot: life will unfold with greater ease, relationships will become more harmonious and fulfilling, and a sense of divine connection will infuse the air you breathe. Whether you are primarily a physical, emotional, mental, natural, spiritual, or shamanic empath, by putting these tools to use in your life, you will soon master the profound spiritual gifts of empathy.

CHAPTER 5

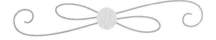

Tools for Compassionate Empathy

*Remember, if you ever need a helping hand, you'll
find one at the end of your arm. As you grow older
you will discover that you have two hands: one for
helping yourself, the other for helping others.*

SAM LEVENSON

The empathic gifts described in chapter 1—all the clairs you read about there—are wonderful tools for connecting with the world around you, but learning to use them can be confusing. You might tend to be sympathetic rather than empathetic, for example. Or you could be susceptible to any of the other experiences that masquerade as empathy listed in chapter 3, such as personalization or emotional contagion. Perhaps you inadvertently shut down some of your empathic gifts or you only feel comfortable using those that make up your strongest empathic style. Maybe you fit into one of the clinical categories of individuals with impaired empathy or you are in a relationship with an impaired empath and don't know what to do.

The good news is that no matter where your empathic gifts lie on the continuums of accessibility and compassionate usefulness, you can develop them. You can make them stronger and more beneficial for yourself and others. The goal of this chapter is to provide you with three basic but vital tools that will help you accomplish all of these aims: to call forth, apply, and even heal your empathic gifts. With these tools at hand, you will be able to discern

- whether to relate to another's empathically communicated need
- if you decide to do so, whether to respond with action or radiant empathy
- whether to relate to impaired empaths

You will have a chance to use these three basic tools throughout the rest of part II, but now it's time to receive them. Open them as you might open three presents that have been carefully beribboned and tinsel-wrapped just for you, for they are gifts that you can use forever.

The Three Primary Tools: The Empath's Medicine Bag

There are three techniques I use all the time, both personally and in my intuitive healing practice. I teach them to classes and clients and describe versions of them in my books. In fact, they are the primary tools I use for establishing boundaries, dealing with challenging situations, and opening to divine guidance. Here I have customized them for the purpose of cultivating empathy. They are as follows:

1. Spirit-to-Spirit
2. Healing Streams of Grace
3. Five Steps to Compassionate Empathy

As you read through these techniques, I invite you to think of ways you can put them to work in your life right away. They come fully alive when practiced.

Tool #1: Spirit-to-Spirit

This is my favorite technique, the result of twenty-five years of cross-cultural study, shamanic studies in other countries, and scholastic research. You can use it for any reason and at any time, and it is an especially useful way to empower yourself empathically.

The technique involves a three-step process that enables you to affirm the highest and most wise part of yourself, affirm the same in others, and then call upon the Greater Spirit, which we call by many names: God, Allah, Christ, the Divine, the Mother, the Holy Spirit, or a Higher Power.

STEP 1: *Affirm Your Own Spirit*

Your spirit is your essence, the spark of the Divine that you are. When you decide to interact empathically from your spirit, you automatically come from your personal best. You also activate the part of you that can make the most effective and loving decisions about empathy: what to pick up on (or not) as well as how to respond. By anchoring your empathic processes in your own spirit, you also include yourself in the equation. The Divine would never decree that you receive an empathic message or respond to intuitive information that is harmful to you.

> *The easiest way to affirm your spirit is to breathe deeply and concentrate on your heart. Your heart is the center of your energetic anatomy, your home of love, and the easiest place through which to access unconditional intelligence. Simply say within yourself, "I affirm that my spirit is in charge of my empathic process."*

STEP 2: *Affirm Others' Spirits*

Everyone—and everything—is an expression of the Divine, including you. Through this step you acknowledge the inner goodness and insight of another person, a group of people, natural forces or beings, entities or angels, or anything else, for that matter. You can even connect with your invisible helpers if you are alone.

> *To affirm others' spirits, simply breathe into your own heart and ask the Divine to tap into the spirits, seen and unseen, who can work toward the highest goal. Then say or think, "I call on the highest spirit of all involved in this empathic process."*

STEP 3: *Affirm the Presence of the Greater Spirit*

This step humbles us. It states that we are setting aside our egos and asking that the Divine—and only the Divine—provide us the empathic information, guidance, and suggestions for actions we need to take. Through this step we put aside our personal agendas and give permission for the Divine to manage all aspects of the empathic process, including providing others and ourselves with protection and healing.

> *To affirm the Greater Spirit, simply believe that the Divine is completely present and give permission for the Divine to take charge of the process you are involved in. Promise to follow the Divine's lead, and know that all will be well.*

You can use Spirit-to-Spirit in many ways—by itself or integrated with the other techniques described in this chapter—and I will teach you how to do this. Here are a few suggestions for how to apply it as a stand-alone technique.

- Start your morning with Spirit-to-Spirit. After invoking the Greater Spirit, ask that it manage your empathic process for that day.
- If you feel as if your empathic boundaries are slipping—that you are becoming too sympathetic or falling prey to another empathy masquerade—use Spirit-to-Spirit. As you affirm the presence of the Divine with the third step, ask

the Greater Spirit to clear the energy that is not your own and rebalance your system.

- If you want to deliberately use your empathic gifts, decide what compassionate action to take, either through your physical presence or by using your radiant empathy abilities. Use all three steps and ask Spirit to show you what to do when you reach the third step.

- If you are with an impaired empath and are feeling stressed or confused, quickly conduct Spirit-to-Spirit, making sure in step 2 that you affirm the impaired empath as well as your invisible helpers. In step 3, ask the Divine to show you how best to interact with the impaired empath.

- If you are preparing for an event that triggers overempathy or otherwise impairs your empathic faculties, conduct Spirit-to-Spirit before the event. In step 2, affirm all members of that group or situation as well as your invisible helpers. During step 3, give permission for the Divine to provide you with special protection.

Tool #2: Healing Streams of Grace

In my investigations into the most successful healers across time, I found a common thread: they have all believed in the power of love to heal. Many were actually able to perceive beams or strands of unconditional divine love surrounding a person in need. When these beams of light entered a person, that person would heal or shift. But a person who was unable to recognize or accept these rays of love remained unaffected by the good wishes.

I believe these streams of light represent grace, which I define as "empowered love" or "love in action." Grace is available for everything and everyone, from the tiniest blade of grass to the most exalted of world leaders. It can even be applied to heal our issues of worthlessness and to sway us toward the highest truth of all: that we are completely and at all times connected to our highest source, which wants only the best for us.

The keys to accepting these invisible yet palpable blessings are to feel worthy of unconditional love and to know that love is empowered to create transformation.

As empaths we can feel and sense these streams of grace and use them to help others and ourselves. They are the perfect antidote to feeling over-empathic; as we surround ourselves with streams of grace, we elegantly establish appropriate boundaries. They are the answer to a call to help others, as we can send healing on a wave of blessed kindness. We've only to ask the Divine to share streams of grace with us to prosper from their assistance.

These are more than "energies." I believe they are bands of consciousness emanating from the Divine that will perform the will of the Highest One for us. While I usually apply these streams of grace for healing and protection, you can also use them for intuitive and empathic protocols, including radiant empathy. The protocol for opening to streams of grace is easy—it, too, is just three steps:

STEP 1: *Ask the Divine to Provide You with Streams of Grace*

I usually use Spirit-to-Spirit first so that I know I'm in a self-loving, open place. I then request, usually through my heart, that the Divine open me (or anyone else) to any and all streams of grace needed at this time. I usually ask that the Divine deliver this grace in such a way as to override any resistance, assisting the parts of self or other that are both willing and not willing to change. (People are usually unwilling to accept love if they feel unworthy or undeserving, for example, and assisting in areas of such resistance invites a healing of the deeper wounds and issues.)

STEP 2: *Accept with Gratitude*

Gratitude is a big yes to grace, most often shouted silently. It also invokes a humble attitude and acquiescence to the Divine rather than personal will.

STEP 3: *Give Permission for the Streams to Shift*

As time goes on, these bands of energy, which psychically appear as various shapes and colors of light, will finish their job. You can ask the Divine to remove the streams of grace that have done their work and continue to adjust streams that should continue working, controlling the intensity and strength of these remaining streams of grace until they, too, are automatically released.

How can you apply streams of grace to empathy and radiant empathy? Following are several ideas. I recommend you always begin these applications having already completed all three steps of Spirit-to-Spirit, as this will assure a healthy attitude and clarity of purpose.

- Ask that the Divine bring only the empathic energy you should receive on streams of grace. This assures that the energy is filtered to be beneficial and healthy for you.

- If you are dealing with an impaired empath, ask the Divine to put a buffer of grace between you and this person so you can remain detached but loving. You can also ask to have yourself and the other person surrounded with healing streams of grace. This is a way to "let go and let God."

- When deciding how to interpret an empathic insight, ask for a healing stream of grace to be provided that will encourage correct interpretation.

- When deciding how to respond to an empathic impulse, ask the Divine to drench your compassionate actions in grace so they result in only positive outcomes.

- If you are or have been too sympathetic, ask the Divine to assist you in registering empathic energies rather than absorbing and holding them. Then request that the Divine carry any internalized energies out of you on a healing stream of grace, taking them where the Divine decrees they should be.

Tools for Compassionate Empathy 109

- When sending radiant empathy, start by clarifying your intention. If you are a physical empath, do you want to send physical healing? If a dark force invades someone, do you desire to free them of this entity? Ask for a healing stream of grace to infuse your intention and carry love to the person, animal, place, object, or situation involved. Be willing to release the outcome, however; healing streams of grace are best used for higher purposes, not personal will.

President Barack Obama once shared some lovely words that I think mirror the combined use of Spirit-to-Spirit and healing streams of grace: "But what we can do, as flawed as we are, is still see God in other people, and do our best to help them find their own grace."[44]

This might be "all we can do," but it is often enough.

Tool #3: Five Steps to Compassionate Empathy

Sometimes we have to be really methodical about how we use our empathic gifts. This is especially true when we want to perform healing, apply our empathy to specific purposes, use radiant empathy, respond to another's need, break an empathic pattern such as pity or sympathy, or work with our own or another's empathic impairment. Under these situations we can use the following five steps:

STEP 1: *Acknowledge the Empathic Information*

You can't effectively decide what to do with empathic information until you have acknowledged you are receiving it. You may have already completed Spirit-to-Spirit when the information comes to you, or you may do Spirit-to-Spirit right after you realize you are getting empathic information. See "How Do You Know It's Empathy?" on page 112 to help you figure out whether you are receiving empathic data and, if so, what type it is.

STEP 2: *Conduct a Compassionate Assessment and Ask for Assistance*

Once you sense you are receiving empathic information, you must determine its message and meaning. You also have to decide whether you should be sitting in the recipient's seat and whether to respond or not. Both activities require the application of compassion—toward the other as well as yourself.

There are two phases to this step, both of which are necessary to assure that you frame the information correctly and with the right personal boundaries.

Phase 1: Sense the importance of this information to the other(s) involved. Empathy involves grasping what an event or situation means to the other, not to ourselves.

Phase 2: Sense how your inner self feels about this data. There are many aspects that might respond to empathic data, including your soul, mind, spirit, and even inner child. Some parts of you are healthy and can deal with almost anything. Some are wounded. It might be injurious for you to interact with certain threads of empathic data. For instance, someone might be dealing with memories of sexual abuse and trigger your own memories of abuse. If you find yourself reacting in phase 2, you have several choices:

- ask for healing streams of grace for yourself
- ask for the empathic information to be blocked (even if temporarily) and to know what to say to the other if communication is necessary
- pause and do the deeper work you need to do before helping or responding to another
- ask the Divine to surround your wounded self in healing streams of grace and promise to help this self later (then do so)

You can now continue to see what the empathic information is telling you.

STEP 3: *Ask for Divine Response*

This step is critical and is sometimes easy to skip. Before you do anything to respond to a perceived need with external action, ask the Divine to serve that need. The Divine might send a healing stream of grace, do nothing, or tell you what you should do, either practically or by means of radiant empathy. Any action you take will be more powerful and beneficial if the Spirit moves first.

STEP 4: *Take Action with Humility*

At this point, you might sense that compassion will involve taking action. Sometimes the action is focused outward and sometimes it might involve prayer, sending a healing stream of grace, or even shifting your own attitude. Humility is key to refusing the temptation to "play God" and think you can fix someone else's life all by yourself. Remember that you are a part of the play, not the only actor.

STEP 5: *Surrender the Outcome*

Whether or not you take an action (outwardly or inwardly), the last step involves surrendering. To surrender involves serving as a witness to another's change while not taking on the responsibility for that change. For instance, you might be led to give money to someone who has no food, but you don't know if that gesture will provide them everything they need or merely fill a hole. Surrendering will help you steer clear of sympathy, emotional contagion, and all other energetic forms of codependency that can keep you hooked into a plight that isn't yours to shoulder.

How Do You Know It's Empathy?

Sometimes it can be hard to figure out whether you're receiving empathic information or manipulative messages or tuning in to your own thoughts, feelings, and memories. Following are some general guidelines about empathic information that can assist you with discernment.

- Empathic information seems to come from outside you and has a quality of transmission that insists that it's not your data. In fact, the vibrational tone of this information will be dissimilar to that of your own thoughts, sensations, and feelings.

- Healthy empathic information will be calm, while manipulative instruction will compel or force you to do its bidding.

- When bodily empathic information is accompanied by clairvoyant or clairaudient data, you can recognize it as distinct from clairvoyance or clairaudience because it is sensory, palpable, and inclusive of energy that changes or affects your feelings, thoughts, or bodily awareness.

- True empathic information will help you feel unified with or attuned to someone else's life or situation but will not overwhelm you, as sympathetic information easily can. You will remain present and whole even while you are experiencing another's reality.

- Manipulative empathy will lead you to forget your own self or needs; you may have a difficult time performing phase 2 of step 2 of the five steps to compassionate empathy, which is focused on self-compassion. You will want to jump in immediately and fix external problems yourself (pity), get caught up in the fray (emotional contagion), pretend to understand what is happening or that you are currently empowered to change it (imagination), remain in phase 2/step 2 and concentrate only on your own reactions (personalization), or avoid step 5 altogether—surrendering the outcome—and assume that everything will be okay no matter what (hyperoptimism).

- Empathic information can wait if it needs to. You have time to get your bearings, pause, and ask for divine assistance.

- If you feel like you are being manipulated, you can always perform Spirit-to-Spirit and ask for assistance or use healing streams of grace as a buffer. The streams of grace can also pull manipulative energy out of you if you request it.

Promptings of Empathy:
How to Recognize Divine Guidance

Sometimes you don't know if you're receiving spiritual guidance or not—an all-important factor in accessing the Divine when using our three techniques. In general, however, all divine messages, whether sent directly from the Divine or delivered by a divinely appointed messenger, are loving and kind. You might feel frightened by the content of the communiqué—if you're receiving a warning of an imminent accident, for example—but the messenger does not scare or threaten you.

Yes, we can receive empathically delivered messages from otherworldly beings. These can include angels, deceased relatives, being from the natural world such as fairies, and other spiritual entities. They can empathically sense what we are going through and respond to us. As well, through our empathic senses, we can feel what they are sensing and respond to them. For instance, my spiritual guides often communicate care, concern, or compassion to me. Unfortunately, there are otherworldly beings whose motives are dark or negative. They can prey on the unprotected or unaware person and absorb our energy or send harmful or inaccurate sensations to us.

Divine revelations, unlike harmful ones, never bulldoze or shame you. They are respectful toward all concerned and encourage respectful behavior. A divine memorandum also aligns with our commonly held set of universal ethics. There is no verbiage implying that you'll go to hell if you don't follow the bullet points, and there are no hidden clauses. You will never be asked to kill or cause injury to self or other. In other words, you can follow divine instruction with a clear conscience.

There are methods for sensing divine guidance that are unique to each of the empathic styles. Knowing these can help you sift through the empathically related messages or sensations you receive and figure out which are divinely approved.

Physical Empathy

If you are a physical empath, the Divine speaks to you by sending sensations into your body. These sensations might be knocks, aches, touches, jarring sensations, gentle taps, or even aromas and tastes. For instance, the Divine might warn you of impending disaster by freezing your movements or alert you to a potential car accident by making you feel as if you are already in one. The Divine could tell you to turn left at the next stoplight by applying pressure to your left hand. As well, you could receive messages from the Divine through the external world. A person with a broken arm might talk with you at a store; you sense their pain but also get the impression that the same could happen to you if you aren't careful.

Emotional Empathy

The Divine communicates with emotional empaths through feelings, stirring emotions, and urges that help you know what to pay attention to and what to do.

Every feeling actually holds its own meaning and provides a certain set of instructions. Joyous feelings affirm, telling you to keep doing what you're doing or to celebrate what is occurring. You can embrace and follow signs or omens that bring you joy without doubt or further analysis. Sadness encourages you to look for the love underlying a perceived loss, and anger says it's time to set boundaries. Fear suggests that you think through an action or idea, preparing yourself to do something different, while disgust insists that something or someone is bad for you. Guilt asks you to examine your own agendas and behaviors, and shame shouts that you are stuck in feelings of unworthiness that should be cleared. (You can use the "Self-Healing for Empaths" exercise on page 122 to help you heal shame.)

Mental Empathy

The code word for a mental empath is *knowing*—the gut sense that tells you what to pay attention to. If you are a mental empath, the Divine will send you messages that leave you with a sense of understanding in your body. Essentially, mental empathy is the mind-body connection in action. Your stomach might tighten if a situation or person is bad for you, or butterflies might start leaping in response to an idea that is accurate.

The key to comprehending these messages is to slow down, breathe, and consciously raise these sensations up your spine to your mind so that you can better understand them. In fact, I suggest that mental empaths ask the Divine to translate their body-based knowing into words, songs, or sounds that can be spoken aloud or written down. Many mental empaths have the gift of clairaudience and can turn their intuitive knowledge into words, and it is good to practice this. Because of this affiliation with clairaudience, you might receive messages through physical reality that are spoken by others, blared over the radio or television, or read in books. You will feel a tingly sensation when these communiqués pertain to you.

Natural Empathy

Nature constitutes a significant expression of the Divine and is a playground for divine creativity. As a natural empath, you can receive inspiration or direct messages from the Divine through any or all natural phenomena or beings.

For instance, animal lovers often receive messages from animals that appear in dreams or even in waking life. Each species in the animal kingdom represents a different concept of reality, which means that if a flock of crows appears outside your window cawing away, it would be wise to figure out what crows signify and pay attention to that theme. (There are many books about the meaning of power animals or totems, as they are often called. You can always Google "the spiritual meaning of …" when researching.) Because crows herald change, for example, when they are unusually present, you know that change is on the horizon.

Individual natural beings can carry personal messages as well. For instance, whenever I'm feeling scared when I'm traveling, a dog will appear out of nowhere to help me. I was once on a trip visiting fifty stone circles throughout the British Islands. Several of these circles were literally in the middle of nowhere—truly—surrounded only by sheep, cows, and sleeting rain. I was often frightened, and each time I was, a dog appeared and remained with me while I tromped around. At least ten such times, the dogs were white with a blue and a brown eye. I am told that dogs with two differently colored eyes can see into the natural world and also the mystical planes.

Other natural forces can hold messages or deliver divine signs as well. A blowing wind can seemingly force you off a path, only to set you on the correct one. A sudden sunbeam can transform into a spotlight showing you where to walk. I was once about to enter a friend's house when I found it suddenly drenched with rain from a cloud that was only releasing on *that* house. I decided to visit that friend on a different day.

Many shamanic empaths are also highly gifted natural empaths, and because of this they can interact with the otherworldly aspects of nature, not only the 3-D versions. If you have both gifts, it is helpful to know a bit more about the supernatural beings that might intermingle with you. In general, paranormal beings from nature come from these three worlds:

- *Beings of the underworld* include fairies, brownies, elves, and nymphs that are associated with magical thresholds (such as caves, lakes, and oceans) and various elemental beings (such as the spirits associated with fire, stone, air, water, earth, metal, wood, light, ether, and star). Also living here are our ancestors and the *Daoine Sidhe*, the Gaelic term for the underworld gods and goddesses.

- *Beings of the middle world* include spirits of trees and plants, animals, reptiles, some birds, and the spirits of our mortal kin, as well as otherworldly and invisible beings that interact with humans.
- *Beings of the overworld* include the spirits associated with stars, moons, and planets, as well as angels, demons, and spiritual guides. Our ancestors believed that we could receive divine messages from omens and signs in the sky such as meteors, comets, planetary movements, or weather phenomena, as well as from birds because they fly.

The Divine can compel beings from any and all of these realms to provide the naturally based shamanic empath with insights, healing, and information.

Spiritual Empathy

The spiritual empath is equivalent to a sensor that responds to various moods of shadow and brightness. Your body actually plays the part of the sensor, registering spiritual information without the intense physical jarring experienced by the physical empath, the emotional wash of the emotional empath, or the mentalism of the mental empath. You simply know what the Divine thinks, believes, or is communicating through the ineffable presence of grace.

The best way to confirm you are receiving a message from the Divine is to trust only those sensations that are accompanied by a feeling of unity with the Divine. Many spiritual empaths rely on the powers of prayer, meditation, and contemplation to provide them with this discernment. Prayer involves talking to the Divine, meditation is receiving messages from the Divine, and contemplation involves basking in the presence of the Divine. When you are accomplishing all three activities at once, you are truly in flow with the Divine and can trust all communications you receive.

Many spiritual empaths also attune to the clairvoyant abilities, receiving images, pictures, and colors in relation to their revelation. This gift of sight can help you interpret the exact message the Divine is communicating.

Shamanic Empathy

The shaman might receive messages in all of the ways I have already described. The distinguishing feature of the shaman is that the Divine often employs mystical dimensions to deliver messages.

Nearly every religion or spiritual tradition is based on shamanic influences. The Christian, Islamic, and Jewish holy books are replete with prophets who deliver information from God to the people through visions, dream interpretation, divining tools, channeling or clairaudience, and interactions with angels or the deceased. They also feature healers, depending on the tract, including Elijah, Elisha, Moses, and Jesus, who perform seeming feats of magic.

This supernatural sphere is the realm of the shaman, who can pluck the Divine's directives from the wind and then turn and summon a spirit to perform healing upon someone. Likewise, the shaman can hear God in the fluttering of a dragonfly's wings and predict an oncoming storm. Because of the breadth and scope of this interactivity, the shamanic empath, more than any other empath, must be truly cautious when discerning whether a message has come from the Divine or is, instead, a willy-nilly comment from a passerby spirit or an insertion from a dark force. I recommend that shamans continually center their consciousness in their hearts, the inner haven of grace, and ask the Divine to announce itself with a particular mantra or sound, vision, or touch of the spirit. If the message is loving and this code is triggered, the shaman can be surer of its divine origin.

No matter our particular type(s) of empathic gift, we can make daily use of the essential tools shared in this chapter. Upon rising, I conduct Spirit-to-Spirit, asking the Greater Spirit to hold me in goodness so I can be of service throughout the day. Immediately upon sensing another's mood, plight, or need, I engage Spirit-to-Spirit again, even if I'm in a queue at the bank or at my son's baseball game. I ask what I am to do with what I'm aware of, if anything. Sometimes I am called to follow through on each of the five steps to compassionate empathy, then to go all out and speak a word, offer assistance, or say a prayer. Yet other times I attend to myself, requesting that the Divine handle a situation via healing streams of grace. And always, I concentrate on the final of these five steps: surrendering. To surrender is to acknowledge that sometimes it is enough to simply sense, feel, or know, and that something greater will take care of the rest.

These three special techniques will serve you well in your personal and professional life and also play a vital role in healing, the act and art of transformation. If to heal is to make whole, which is the subject of the next chapter, empathy is key to recognizing that wholeness already exists, whether we are currently able to perceive it or not.

CHAPTER 6

Empathic Healing: How Empaths Can Heal Themselves and Others

*We don't set out to save the world; we set out to
wonder how other people are doing and to reflect
on how our actions affect other people's hearts.*

PEMA CHÖDRÖN

Empathy compels us to help the people, beings, or forces that slip through our boundaries and summon our compassion. Sometimes the call to help overwhelms us, and we end up struggling. Should we assist another or not? Are we capable of doing so or not?

At other times, the urge to provide help comes from within and is directed toward ourselves. Some part of our body, mind, or soul is held hostage to a past trauma, addiction, or problem, and we must turn our eye inward and, from a place of love, send love and healing.

This chapter addresses the deep desire that lies within all empaths, no matter the style of gift: to provide healing or insight to another or to ourselves. We will apply the three empathic techniques we learned in chapter 5 toward this endeavor, looking at how to ease all kinds of afflictions, from false empathy to physical challenges.

This important knowledge speaks to the soul of the empath, who at some level is asked to take up the torch of healer.

The Empathic Healer

Georgia came to see me because she could sense everyone's deeper wounds. "I need only sit next to someone at a business meeting, and I come away worrying about them," she related. "I am especially aware of the emotional damage caused by their childhoods. And believe me, almost everyone is damaged."

Georgia expressed that her biggest challenge was figuring out what to do. "I don't know if I should say something or ignore the problems. I try to send prayers, but I don't think it does any good.

"Most of the time I simply do nothing," she sighed. "But that doesn't feel right either. Why would I know what's up if I wasn't supposed to do something?"

Why, indeed? Nearly every type of empath has asked me this question in one form or another:

- Why do I have to know that the dog next door is being neglected if there is nothing I can do about it?
- Why do I have to feel every change of barometric pressure before it occurs?
- Why do I only have to touch someone's hand to sense every pain in their body?
- Why do I have to know when someone is dishonest— especially if confronting them will get me fired/cause a divorce/create family friction?

- Is it really my job to see every bloody entity attached to someone? How helpful is that really, since if I say anything people will call me crazy?

There are two additional questions I frequently hear, usually in reference to impaired empathy:

- Do I really have to be such a sucker? I swear my empathy does nothing but get me taken advantage of.
- How come I'm so different from everyone else? My empathic impairment only causes me frustration and loss.

While empathy is touted as the force that will save the world and bond us together like a knot in a shoelace, being empathic isn't easy. Quite simply, it's hard to figure out what we're getting, what it means, and what exactly we're supposed to do about it—especially if the incoming information relates to healing needs. This is where the tools I introduced in the last chapter can be of tremendous help.

But before we can apply the three empathic tools to healing, we must first have a firm grasp of the concept of healing—what it is and what we can expect from healing processes, whether they involve tangible action or radiant empathy. I've determined that most empaths, even certain types of impaired ones, usually expect too much of themselves, and this must be cleared up before they can become effective empathic healers.

What Is Healing Really?

Empaths spend much of their time engaged in healing and often don't even know it. The word *healing* means "to make whole." It is the process of helping someone return to a more whole state than they are in now or even achieve a more whole state than they have ever enjoyed.

When we're in need of healing—whether our discomfort is physical, financial, relational, emotional, mental, or spiritual—we usually concentrate on relieving symptoms. We don't like feeling sick or sad, poor or unloved, stupid or in pain. Why would we? No one does. Therefore, the first and foremost goal is a reprieve.

As instinctive as this drive is, the problem is that healing isn't equivalent to an immediate or even eventual shift of symptoms. We can heal while having cancer and still die from the disease. We can heal poverty issues and continue to overwork for a subsistence wage. Likewise, we can provide someone else healing yet see little change in the way their dilemmas appear.

This fact grates on most empathic people. When we attune to another's hardship, we feel or know their agony, grief, or hurt. They aren't the only one going through pain; we feel it also. Why wouldn't we want to provide an immediate release?

Sometimes we sense that someone else is enjoying him- or herself or having a good day. Most of us like noticing that others are happy. Sensing that someone else is satisfied or that their life is pleasant doesn't usually impel a call to heal. This isn't true for certain types of impaired empaths, who often get angry when others are happy. Individuals with narcissism and other personality disorders, PTSD, and even schizophrenia or other psychospiritual challenges might become jealous of the joy others can achieve because it seems out of reach to them. We can all imagine struggling with difficulties that would make us so envious of others' happiness that we wish the worst on them.

The urge to relieve ourselves or others of discomfort, whether the distress occurs because someone else is dismayed or overjoyed, is a major cause of empathic difficulties. To alleviate our uneasiness, we might anxiously gulp in another's energy or fake our reaction, exhibiting emotional contagion. We might deny our doubt about a healing and fall into hyperoptimism or reach out in pity and get stuck with someone else's problems. If we're dealing with a malevolent impaired empath, we might fall prey to their shaming or manipulation. If we're autistic or have ADHD, we might become overstimulated and lose focus.

The truth is that healing energies may or may not provide immediate relief; we cannot predict results. All we are assured is that if we follow the Divine's compassionate lead, we will help ourselves and others achieve the highest possible outcome. Ultimately, the healing process is dependent on acknowledging that we are powerless to alleviate the suffering of another. We can help, care, assist, or advise, but the work of transformation depends on the Divine. And, ironically, the more we get out of the way, the more powerfully the Divine can assert itself.

The importance of opening the gate to the Divine is apparent in the following example. Consider a natural empath who is attuned to a baby animal whose mother isn't around at that moment. She might sense that this baby is scared and worried. It would be natural to try to soothe or pet the baby. How wise is this if we're talking about a bear cub and Mom could be right around the corner? Rather than trying to alleviate her empathic discomfort through a knee-jerk reaction, our natural empath could use our three empathic tools to invite divine assistance.

Let's imagine our empath conducts Spirit-to-Spirit and senses that the mom is nearby and it's safe (if not safer) to leave. Maybe she sends healing streams of grace to the baby, using radiant empathy, and the grace calms the baby. Perhaps she even sends healing streams of grace to the mom, which carry the message "hurry back." Maybe she conducts the full five steps to compassionate empathy and calls a forest ranger or an expert to help, surrendering to the fact that she can't fix every problem by herself. It's always helpful to invite the Divine into the process, knowing that in doing so we might not immediately ease our discomfort, but we will be led to the best solution to the problem.

The remainder of this chapter will further this discussion as we look at the processes involved in healing self and others.

Self-Healing for Empaths

There are many circumstances in which we feel compelled to heal ourselves. Maybe we've triggered PTSD by sensing another's situation empathically or we have fallen into the trap of one of the many empathic masquerades. We might be aware that our empathy is blocked. Or we might simply want to use our empathic gifts to invite physical, emotional, mental, or another type of healing for ourselves.

Following is a process you can undertake for any reason to help free your empathic self for greater health and well-being. Step 3 showcases a few ways you can customize this process to your special type of empathy, your primary empathic style.

PREPARATION: *Conduct Spirit-to-Spirit*

Affirm your inner spirit, the spirit in all others, and the presence of the Greater Spirit.

STEP 1: *Ask for and Acknowledge Needed Information*

Request that the Divine help you understand the reason for your challenge. Ask to be shown the reasons for your current difficulties, and ask that you be held and protected while you perceive what occurred.

STEP 2: *Conduct Compassionate Self-Assessment and*
Ask for Divine Assistance

This step asks you to embrace and shift the misperceptions that led to your challenges.

First, ask the Divine to help you perceive yourself with compassion, as if you are wearing eyeglasses that shine with forgiveness and light while probing for the beliefs that led you to adopt an empathic strategy that hasn't benefited you. Is there anything you need to say or share with your wounded self? Is there a need for a healing stream of grace to assist or protect this inner self?

Second, ask the Divine to assist you with seeing into the hearts of the others who were involved in the situation that is still causing you difficulties. What were they really going through? What challenges were they trying to cope with? Why might they have interacted with you in such a way as to cause you harm?

When you feel like you've achieved a sense of compassion for yourself and others, you can move on.

STEP 3: *Ask for Divine Response*

Now ask the Divine to provide full healing for you and any others involved in the situation. Take your time with each stage of this healing. You might need to give yourself days or weeks to concentrate fully on your own inner self and a similar amount of time to achieve peace with others. Know that the Divine can reach out to you in any number of ways, depending on your empathic style. A physical empath might feel compelled to eat certain foods or exercise in a new way, while an emotional empathy could receive an abundance of emotional support from friends. A mental empath could be hit on the head with a book full of guidance or instruction, while a natural empath might receive boons from the birds. A spiritual empath could receive signs directly from the Greater Spirit, and a shaman from angels visiting in dreams. It is common for the Divine to reach us through our strongest empathic gift, so it is important to pay attention to what occurs in and around you after you've asked for divine assistance.

STEP 4: *Take Action with Humility*

During this stage, ask the Divine if there are any further actions you should take to bolster your healing. These actions might be concrete, such as seeking additional therapy or getting help with an addiction. Or they may involve radiant empathy, which could entail continually checking in on an "inner child" so he or she knows your adult self is present. Actions are often multilayered; we take one step forward and are then asked to take another. Because change often occurs in a process, not because of a single behavior, we have to continually self-assess, asking ourselves whether we feel like there could be further transformation to allow. We can always ask the Divine if there is more for us to do or accomplish—and for encouragement so that we can keep moving in the right direction.

In this step you can also ask the Divine to provide healing streams of grace to all concerned, including current-life and past-life parts of yourself. These streams can be used to replace dysfunctional beliefs with accurate ones, soothe inflamed emotions, or substitute a divine connection for energetic or entity attachments. Ask, too, that all soul issues be addressed. How about allowing the Divine to retrieve the parts of you that have been lost over time and to return the parts of others that have adhered themselves to you? Remember also to request a shift in your epigenes or ancestral codes or any other aspect of self that requires assistance.

You can then ask if you need to perform radiant empathy for yourself. Yes, we can send healing to ourselves, using our particular empathic gift to share physical, emotional, mental, spiritual, or nature-based energies with our wounded self. A shamanic empath can ask for otherworldly assistance as well.

STEP 5: *Surrender the Outcome*

What exactly do we surrender when we perform self-healing? We don't know what our healed—or continually healing—state will look like. We might want to think that the shy self, shamed for her empathic style, will suddenly develop the confident demeanor of a bold and colorful socialite; she might not. We might believe that our overbearing style will relax and we'll be easier for others to get along with. Maybe, maybe not; perhaps other changes will occur first. We become comfortable with our shy attitude and start writing books at night. We transform our aggressiveness into the ability to stand up for others. There will be changes—good changes; we simply need to notice them.

When Seeking to Heal Others

Sometimes we feel empathically led to assist others. We like it when the message to act is clear and we can proceed. But life isn't always so convenient, and that's why I describe the steps for healing others from the starting place of attuning to an external empathic call—or cry—for help. By following these steps, you will give yourself multiple opportunities to discern a fork in the road that will empower you to make a decision: whether to help others or dismiss yourself from that work with clarity and confidence.

Initial Contact: You've Received a Message

A person, situation, natural being, or spirit reaches out to you and compels a healing response, whether they do so consciously or not. With all of our discussions about empathy to this point under your belt, you are now better equipped to consider the following critical factors:

- whether you are the correct recipient for this awareness or not
- whether it's beneficial for you to receive this information or not
- whether you are able to empathize instead of sympathizing, thereby avoiding any of these pitfalls: imagining a response, falling into emotional contagion, pitying or personalizing, being hyperoptimistic, or supporting an unhealthy, impaired empath
- whether you are called to respond, either through concrete action or radiant empathy (I deal with this step later in this section)

Different empathic styles will figure out the best responses to the first three points in different ways, as follows:

PHYSICAL EMPATHS: Sensing others' physical issues can be startling and leave you wondering whether the pain you feel is your own or another's. If the physical sensations are overbearing, excruciating, or don't release when you ask for divine help, you are stuck in a masquerade and need to ask the Divine to release you with a healing stream of grace. Proceed only if you can refrain from believing yourself to be a miracle maker, and you'll be okay with what might appear to be a non-outcome.

EMOTIONAL EMPATHS: The other's emotional pain or feelings will fit you like a lock and key and cause no reaction other than compassion. If your own issues are stimulated, you will be able to clearly differentiate the other's energy from your own. You won't feel burdened or more intensely stimulated, as you would if your reaction was sympathetic, nor will you be tempted to take advantage of the other's emotions to express your own. And you will not have the sense that you have to help no matter what.

MENTAL EMPATHS: If the data you've received is destined for you, you can embrace it calmly and cleanly. Don't proceed if instead you feel forced into a response, nauseous, or overanxious. Know that your own awareness cannot fix another's issues.

NATURAL EMPATHS: You can proceed with your empathic steps if you feel a sense of peace about participating. If the empathic calling is unhealthy for you, you might feel stressed and worried. Negative reactions to environmental stressors such as mold, inorganic materials, chemicals, additives, or electromagnetic fields might increase, and you could find yourself obsessing over the need to help.

SPIRITUAL EMPATHS: An affirmative "proceed" will be accompanied by the sense of being unified with the Divine. Ask to be cleared of the empathic information if instead you feel despairing, anxious, depressed, or have a sense of foreboding or darkness. If you feel shaky or cold, you might have already taken on the other's negative energies and need to ask the Divine to clear you.

There is one additional warning sign for the spiritual empath in regard to reacting to impaired empaths. While they can appear quite charming and enchanting, if not downright enlightened, in actuality they are highly manipulative. You will feel sick to your stomach no matter how they appear. At some level the person is asking you to ignore your spiritual truthfulness and buy into their appearance. Ask the Divine to send them a healing stream of grace and dismiss you from service.

SHAMANIC EMPATHS: One of the major liabilities of being a shamanic empath is the continual receptivity to empathic needs. Think of how many beings from dozens of worlds can potentially reach out for help.

Being a shaman necessitates strong energetic boundaries, which can be formed by asking the Divine to surround you with an abundance of healing streams of grace. If you ask the Divine for this protection and it doesn't stabilize, perform self-healing; there might be internal reasons for this or interference from dark forces.

I also recommend that you appoint a gatekeeper to help oversee your empathic causes. This spiritual protector, which could even be the Divine, will only attune to the empathic messages that are divinely approved. With these healthy defense mechanisms in place, you can proceed to help another if your gatekeeper allows it.

Dismissal: Perform Spirit-to-Spirit and Invoke Grace

It's important to figure out if you are supposed to proceed in a healing capacity or not. Sometimes a person, group, or animal reaches out for help, but it's not for us to respond. They might blindly throw out an SOS or personalize their plea to us. Either way, before going any further, perform Spirit-to-Spirit and ask the Divine to clue you in. Are you really supposed to assist or not? Is there any reason you are supposed to refrain? Unless you are clearly supposed to proceed, don't. Instead, ask the Divine to use healing streams of grace to return the other's data or energy to them.

You can also request a healing stream of grace for yourself. This stream will wash you clean of the other's murky energy. Also request that you be surrounded with a bubble of grace that will serve as a filter. This will help keep you from being reached again by persons or beings that should not be contacting you. If some part of you insists you should help even if doing so would be bad for you, do some self-healing work to figure out why.

If you are clear that you are supposed to provide assistance, move to the next stage, which is to prepare yourself to serve as a healing instrument.

Preparation: Perform Spirit-to-Spirit and Invoke Grace

You believe that you are called to assist another. Let's double-check. Once again, execute Spirit-to-Spirit and ask for another affirmation. Ask yourself if you are supposed to continue. If you receive an affirmation, use the healing streams of grace to surround yourself in a bubble. Know that this bubble, or membrane of grace, directly connects you with the Divine, which will protect, guide, and help you through your healing endeavor. Now you can continue on to step 1.

STEP 1: *Ask for and Acknowledge Further Information*
Ask the Divine to provide information you need to better understand your role as a healer.

STEP 2: *Conduct a Compassionate Assessment and Ask for Assistance*
Now dig deeper to perceive what the Divine wants you to know about another's real needs. What is the nature of the challenge? Are there causal factors you need to be aware of? Is there a word, a treatment, or a type of energy to avoid because it might cause further harm?

Next, concentrate on yourself. We are never called by the Greater Spirit to perform a task that will endanger us. Could you incur potential harm by participating in this healing? If so, ask the Divine if there is an extra layer of protection that you need or if, before proceeding, you need to conduct some self-healing. Ask, too, what will help you register intuitive and energetic information rather than absorb and hold it. Is there a certain way to work that is more rather than less compassionate toward yourself? Is there anything you must first tend to in yourself? This is a good time to ask the Divine for healing streams of grace to soothe, heal, and protect you as you move forward into providing healing for another.

STEP 3: *Ask for Divine Response*

It is now time to ask the Divine to provide the healing for the other. Your role is to witness what the Divine delivers.

STEP 4: *Take Action with Humility*

The Divine might now call you to deliver service. Begin this step by asking the Divine if you are supposed to perform an energetic task such as employing radiant empathy to send a statement or affirmation, or transporting energy; each is best done by containing the energy inside healing streams of grace. You might also sense that you are supposed to both send a message and transport energy. These activities can be "packaged" inside the same healing stream of grace.

Each empathic style will use radiant empathy in a slightly different way:

PHYSICAL EMPATHS: When sending physical healing to another, it's important to remember that you do not send your own personal life energy. This will result in exhaustion, fatigue, and eventually a depressed immune system. Usually, a physical empath sends a healing stream of grace into the part of the body or the chakra that is afflicted. If you are in doubt about where to direct the grace, ask the Divine to deliver the stream of grace to the other person's spirit.

Another technique I often use is to ask the Divine to interweave natural energies—including the vibrations of herbs, tinctures, or even the elements—into the streams of grace. These fortified streams can be programmed to deliver the exact amount and intensity needed and to be discarded when the healing is done.

EMOTIONAL EMPATHS: The healing streams of grace emotional empaths send are most frequently composed of soothing feelings that balance disturbed emotions. Some emotional empaths like to visualize different colors inside the streams. Following is a list of colors with a description of energies you can provide.

- Red energizes and stimulates—ideal for someone who is depressed, exhausted, or despairing. Do not use for someone who is angry, agitated, or stuck in PTSD.

- Orange enhances joy and promotes playfulness. It invites enthusiasm in those who feel drab or overly responsible and shifts us from apathy, or "Who cares?" to empathy, or "I care."

- Yellow promotes mental activity and stimulates awareness. Do not use if anxiety or frustration are present.

- Green encourages tranquility, connectedness, and overall good health.

- Blue soothes and calms and enhances productivity. Do not use if someone is sad or lonely, as blue can increase these feelings.

- Purple encourages wisdom, foresight, and assurance of the future.

- White cleanses and supports a return to innocence and purity.

- Black stimulates repressed grief and actualizes power. It can also call forth the presence of hidden memories, shadow issues, and menacing entities. Use with the utmost discernment.

- Silver deflects negativity and evil and invites transmission of higher truths. It is an excellent color for protection and removal of entities, as well as emotions about the presence of entities.

- Gold represents divine power and enables the manifestation of higher will.

MENTAL EMPATHS: You can package supportive statements and words with healing streams of grace, including statements such as "you are a success" or "you are worthy." These are good antidotes to the negative messages mental empaths often perceive.

NATURAL EMPATHS: What better way to provide healing for nature-based beings than to use the technique just described for physical empaths? Ask the Divine to insert natural medicines, elements, or energies into the streams of grace you direct to the one in need. For example, think of the potency of herbs, the strength of stones, the warmth of fire, and the refreshment of water. Nature contains everything required for healing. You may also draw on the powers of celestial bodies such as the moon, stars, and planets. Many natural empaths respond to others' needs by serving as feng shui masters, designing an environment to be energetically balanced, or seeking solutions in the wisdom of astrology.

SPIRITUAL EMPATHS: Many spiritual empaths deliver a healing stream of grace while praying. You can also visualize the stream as white, the purest and most complete of all colors, or gold, which results in the immediate enforcement of divine will.

SHAMANIC EMPATHS: The shamanic empath can use any of these techniques in addition to one other significant provision: spirits. Why not call upon a nature spirit or a risen master to provide insight as well as healing? Why not ask angels to perform psychic surgery on a tumor or remove an entity from an addict? Shamans can always avail themselves of otherworldly assists.

STEP 5: *Surrender the Outcome*

You are not in charge of the changes others allow for themselves or of what the Divine does for them. Sometimes illness and other challenges are designed for growth, and because of this we won't perceive any healing. At other times, healing is a matter of timing: it is not yet time to see a significant change. And sometimes the transformations that take place are more than skin deep—they occur within another and cannot be perceived externally. Peace is ours when we release ourselves from the position of God.

Is It Your Dilemma?

How do you know whether your empathic abilities are attuning you to your own illness, dilemma, or healing need or to someone else's? After using Spirit-to-Spirit to receive divine guidance, you can employ this simple technique to find out.

Concentrate on the healing need you perceive and then pick up an object. Ask the Divine to help you pour the need into the object. Then set the object down and walk away from it.

If the issue, sensation, or problem seems to persist, chances are that the challenge belongs to you. If it fades or disappears, the trauma or drama might be another's. If less than half of the previous empathic sensation dissipates, the issue might actually belong to someone else but could also be triggering a similar one in you. If this is the case, you'll want to perform self-healing to figure out whether it is better to assist the other or simply release them on a healing stream of grace, asking the Divine to surround them with light and remove their attachment from you with love. When this process is complete, you can also ask the Divine to cleanse the object of your own or another's energy with that same restorative flow of grace.

An Example of Healing: Freedom from PTSD

What might an empathic healing look like when performed? I have included this section to help you embrace yourself as a healer so you can perceive ways in which your empathic gifts might benefit another. It assumes that you are employing the techniques you have just learned.

We are going to focus on PTSD, the trauma-induced state that lingers after a catastrophe, illness, shocking event, or overwhelming loss. I believe that PTSD underlies many impaired empathic challenges, including mental disorders such as anxiety, depression, substance abuse, and more (for further information on this, please see appendix 2). It can be carried from one lifetime to another, applies to soul fragmentation, can be a result of entity attachments, and can even be triggered through our epigenes, or from the state of primary cell development onward.

In order for you to best visualize the application of your empathic healing powers, I want you to imagine that you are in a room with a person (or, in the case of natural empathy, an animal) in need of healing from prior trauma. This means that you can touch or talk with them, depending on your empathic style, although you will primarily be sending energy through radiant empathy. Simply imagine that you are going through these experiences according to your empathic style.

Conduct Spirit-to-Spirit and make sure that you are supposed to proceed. If the process is affirmed, ask Spirit to provide insight about your role as a healer. Is there anything specific you need to know? Is there a certain way you are supposed to work or are there any pitfalls to avoid?

Ask also if there are any divine helpers being assigned to this process. In particular, a natural empath might sense the presence of a natural helper such as a power animal or a plant spirit. You might sense you need to surround yourself with an elemental force such as air, water, stone, metal, wood, fire, ether (higher ideals), earth, star (fire and ether), or light. An entity, ghost, spirit, or angelic being might join a shamanic empath. Any or all empaths will work with the attributes of their personal style but might tap into clairvoyance, clairaudience, or another empathic style as well.

Now ask the Divine to help you assess both the symptoms and causes of the PTSD. The physical empath might actually feel the physical repercussions of both, such as a pain in the shoulder of a veteran who was shot down in battle. An emotional empath might feel the original emotional shock of a friend who found her spouse in bed with another woman, as well as the long-term shame and anger that followed. A mental empath might sense the change in the victim's self-esteem or receive knowledge of what actually occurred during the abusive events.

A natural empath will most likely draw on shamanic tendencies to relate to the physical, emotional, mental, and spiritual sensitivities of an animal companion, perhaps sensing a dog's arthritic hip, feelings of confusion, perception that it's done something wrong to cause the pain, and the Divine's stance that the arthritis can be healed.

As a spiritual empath, you might pick up on the Divine's anger that a person was mistreated or perhaps sexually abused. And as a shaman, you might do all of the above while having a meaty, in-depth conversation with the person's favorite spirit guide.

The Healing Begins

It's almost time to ask the Divine to begin the healing process. First, ask if you need anything specific from the Divine before you continue. In exploring the symptoms and causes of the other person's PTSD, have you triggered any of your own trauma issues? Have you been mistreated in a similar way? If so, ask the Divine for a healing stream of grace and to indicate whether you should continue or not. If you receive a no, gently send a healing stream of grace to the person and suggest that they work with someone else. Explain that you don't feel qualified or ready to help.

If you are to continue, it's time to ask the Divine to assist the person you are striving to help heal. Guess what? Now you get to observe. Feel, listen, see, and sense what is occurring. You might need to talk with the person about what they are currently experiencing or even about the traumatic incident that caused the resulting PTSD. It is during this stage that many recipients of healing think that the healer is doing all the work. Actually, though, the Divine is doing all healing. You might be talking, listening, coaching, or even hugging, but the Divine is delivering the healing energy.

You might sense that you now have a part to play in the healing endeavor. What is your role? What should you do? Let the Divine guide you. Typical activities might include the following:

> PHYSICAL EMPATHS: You feel guided to put your hands
> on the PTSD sufferer and channel through them a healing
> stream of grace. You might even sit across the room and hold
> your hands out, palms toward the person. Or you can hold an
> object, program it with a healing stream of grace, and hand
> it to the person. You might also feel prompted to advise the
> "healee" about specific physical actions to take for their own
> continued healing: seeing a massage therapist, attending a
> twelve-step meeting, running every day, or whatever emerges.

> EMOTIONAL EMPATHS: Your job is to help the person
> express their hidden feelings. You can label the emotions
> you feel in your own body and ask if they're on target. Is the
> person sad? Scared? Angry? Ask what they need in order to
> reveal their feelings to you or to someone else. You can also
> imagine sending healing streams of grace in various colors

into their body to stir and clear emotions. It's best to continue this until the person reaches a mild sense of joy or lightness: relief, gratitude, optimism, or satisfaction, for example. Other feelings are not bad or wrong; they simply indicate that there are more emotions to clear, either now or later.

MENTAL EMPATHS: It's as if you can sense or hear the person's thoughts, specifically those interwoven with the onset of the PTSD. Through your sensitivity, you can surface the negative beliefs that developed because of the trauma: lies like "I am worthless" or "I am powerless." It is actually these misperceptions that cause the recycling of PTSD symptoms, sometimes the intensification of those symptoms, and even impaired empathy and its resulting emotional dramas. Frequently, mental empaths are called upon to help the person reexperience the causal event, coaching them through the persistent pain so as to pinpoint and then shift the dysfunctional beliefs. Using radiant empathy, send the person the appropriate beliefs on healing streams of grace so as to energetically replace the inaccurate ones.

SPIRITUAL EMPATHS: You will be filled with sensations that will help you address and change the misguided shame that always results from being abused or traumatized. In fact, I believe that the glue that binds the repetitive terror, pain, and grief (as well as other shards of emotional fallout from the original ordeal) is shame: the conviction that we are a bad person because something bad happened to us. The terror results from believing that the disturbing event will repeat. Underneath all of these reactions is that toxic theory that the Divine doesn't love us or he or she would have rescued us. As a spiritual empath, you provide primary and primal healing by sharing the truth of the Divine's unconditional love; the person needs to hear this truth in order to heal. If they refuse to believe in their inherent lovability and deservedness, send them the certainty of their worth in a healing stream of grace.

SHAMANIC EMPATHS: You might do any or all of the above in addition to holding court with spirits that can help you remove entity attachments and dark forces. I believe that serious PTSD, especially the kind that results in addictions, chronic anxiety, depression, and other forms of impaired empathy (including narcissism, schizophrenia, and bipolar disorder), almost always involves manipulative dark forces. These "whisper" to their host, prompting negative thoughts and self-destructive behaviors. The easiest way to release an intrusive entity is to substitute a healing stream of grace for the attachment, then ask the Divine to do the rest.

When you've done all you can do, surrender the outcome. Ask the Divine to continue the healing long after the life-affirming interaction you have just experienced has ended.

As we've explored, the urge to help others, to stand in the place of healer, is intertwined with being empathic. To perform healing is a natural expression of our innate compassion, an extension of the loving call to kindness. Still, as much as we'd like to help—as frequently as we are stirred by our own or another's needs—we must always stop and wonder: is this for me to do? Even if we proceed to follow our empathic yearnings, we must remember that our role is most frequently to serve as the witness, the one who cares, allowing the greater healing to be done by the Divine. Our role is not insignificant, however, whether performing healings for self or others. To be empathetic, to sense a need, and to add love to the process of being an instrument of grace are immeasurable gifts that reflect the divinity within our souls.

CHAPTER 7

The Empath in Relationships

*I define connection as the energy that exists between
people when they feel seen, heard, and valued; when they
can give and receive without judgment; and when they
derive sustenance and strength from the relationship.*

BRENÉ BROWN

A few years ago, I overheard two young children sitting in a sandbox. The little boy was crying. I wondered if the girl had taken his beach toys. But no—and I soon heard her ask this:

"Do you know your tears turn into smiles as soon as you get them out?"

"But I feel bad!" the boy wailed.

"I know; I feel it too." The little girl nodded sagely. "So let's both feel sad and then happy together."

The sobs stopped, and pretty soon the two children were playing alongside each other.

This interlude was a telling example of empathy. When two people or beings, no matter their age or background, share with each other, the result is love.

Joy often rises and falls based on this loving empathic connection. We are designed for relationships of all kinds; our empathic wiring is proof of this. We are here to relate, each according to our own ability and style.

The purpose of this chapter is to explore the roles of the various empathic styles in relationships. First we'll look at each empathic style and explore how it enriches close personal relationships, as well as the most typical challenges linked with it. Then we'll address the role that the steps to compassionate empathy can play to better your relationships and solve your empathic problems. Also included, at the end of this chapter, are useful sections showing you how to deal with one of the most vexing (and rampant) relationship issues of our time—narcissism—and how to increase your empathy even if you've been struggling to do so. You can apply all of this information to your most vital relationships, those closest to your heart.

As we journey through this landscape of soul and love, be prepared to both laugh and cry at some of the ways you've experienced empathy with those close to you. As the two youngsters in the sandbox revealed, love really exists where tears and sunshine can comingle.

The Knowing of Love

What makes two people feel close and connected? It starts—and ends—with intimacy, the art of being vulnerable in love. Intimacy is completely dependent on the ability to exchange moods, cares, and awareness. The same is true of creating intimacy with beings of nature and those from the other worlds. Empathy is also core to intimately sensing the information in a crystal stone or the principles illuminated by moving planets. No matter how we bond or what we are bonding with, it is empathy that forms unity. Because of empathy, we can dance in another's shoes and cry when they are sad. Because of empathy, we can love.

Each brand of empathy opens the empath to a unique way of communing through love. And, as with all good things, each empathic style also opens us to certain challenges. As we explore both the ideal and the difficult facets of the various types of empathy, I encourage you to explore whether you have experienced what is described. Search for your yearnings and longings within your heart; these are the soul desires that will tell you where there are horizons yet to be touched, sources of love yet to be enjoyed.

Physical Empathy: The Other within the Self

You may be familiar with *matryoshka*, those Russian nesting dolls: one brightly painted, oval-shaped doll rests inside of another and yet another, and so on. Remove the many layers and you find a tiny child doll nestled inside. In close relationships, a physical empath often functions in a similar fashion. Inside the physical empath lies the physical sensations of another person; inside these are those of yet another person.

In a relationship, physical empaths are usually highly responsible and great providers. After all, they are able to sense others' physical needs, including material provisions such as food, housing, clothing, and financial security.

Many physical empaths attune to these fundamental core requirements, sensing when another is dealing with inadequate material support. Yet others sense other people's physical sensations such as bodily aches, pains, and illnesses. Many physical empaths sense all of the above.

If you are a physical empath, you are most likely one of the best material providers, mates, fathers, or mothers around. Danger occurs when you are folded into a relationship with an irresponsible person who is more than happy to have you to do the work while they cruise. I once spent four years in a relationship with a man who kept telling me he was going to make money and somehow never got around to doing it. Supporting my own two sons, him, and his children was enough to take me down. When I presented a deadline for action, he decided to leave.

That relationship taught me that you simply cannot do for others what they should be doing for themselves, whether it's paying bills or providing healing assistance. Physical empaths often end up with adrenal burnout, fatigue, and illnesses caused by sympathy. The other likely complaint is caregiver burnout or stress, which results from taking on another's problematic symptoms. It is a common occurrence in emotional empaths but an even more serious challenge for physical empaths; despite their outward protestations, they often find themselves partnered with individuals who require assistance or working in jobs with unhealthy people.

The link between physical empathy and caregiver burnout was presented in an academic paper outlining the origins of "compathy"—the shared ("com") feelings ("pathy") of physical empathy. According to the authors of this paper, physically empathic individuals exhibit a "compethic response," which causes one of four scenarios:

- Two people can mirror identical symptoms, and this can make it hard to tell who is really ill.

- Symptoms can also be transferred, such as when a man with a pregnant wife experiences the same back pain and odd food cravings she does.

- A third possibility is called "converted compathy," in which the recipient of the empathic sensations changes the symptoms so as to share healing with the other. For example, as a physical empath I often sense my client's physical problems in corresponding parts of my body. I once sensed a client's newly broken thigh. The pain was quite sharp. As I registered the pain, I had my psyche mute the throbbing hurt into a dull sensation until it was nearly nonexistent. I then used radiant empathy to transfer this slight discomfort to my client, using a healing stream of grace to substitute this much-improved version of pain for the agonizing one. My client immediately sighed and said, "This is a pain I can live with."

- And a fourth possibility is "initiated compathy," which involves one person sending his or her symptoms into someone else.

According to the paper's authors, the beauty of physical empathy is that a caregiver who can truly sense what is occurring in another can provide the optimum care. The problem, as we have seen, is that the empath can become overworked, overburdened, used up, and just plain sick.[45]

We have also discussed the potential for the physical empath to be sensitive to the energy stored in objects. I've experienced the upside and downside of this ability myself. I remember staying at a bed and breakfast one night and not being able to sleep. I felt "bad energy" coming from a desk in the corner. In the morning I discovered that a woman had written a suicide note at that desk. Of course, a physical empath can benefit others using this same ability; you've only to touch someone's hand or favorite object to sense what is occurring in them.

Theoretically, in the case of my sensitivity to the suicidal spirit, I could ask the Divine for assistance to make sure she has "gone to the light" or been sweetly passed to the angels on the "other side." This is true of all such negative or sometimes frightening vibrations. If we open to divine inspiration and help—and put ourselves in the quotient in terms of self-care—we can use all things for good.

Another positive tool for a physical empath is to deliberately program objects given to loved ones, such as presents, with good intentions. You can hold a note whose destination is a kid's lunchbox, a bracelet being presented to a friend, or a gemstone or watch that you've chosen for your partner and use your radiant empathy powers to send blessings into that object, and these will then be shared with your loved one. Simple actions like this are a brilliant way to share your gift.

Emotional Empathy: Magic Markers of Love

Audrey was a typical emotional empath. "My world is an array of colored magic markers, each a different feeling—each a different shade of my inner self," she told me. "I'm so lucky my second husband is an emotive man. We share so much joy. My first marriage was impossible, though. Bob never had a feeling—I had them all.

"In fact," Audrey added, "my first husband thought I was borderline because I was so emotional. It took forever to figure out that I was simply feeling   and expressing—all the emotions my husband refused to acknowledge."

In personal relationships, emotional empaths are just that: people who color life with feelings. They are able to sense what loved ones feel, relate their own emotional needs, and sometimes fill in the emotional caverns in another's soul.

Typically women reveal more skill with emotional empathy and expression than do men, but this is probably a result of culture and modeling. Millennia ago our ancestors assumed a social compact that neatly divided human tasks according to gender. Men were to hunt, women to gather. With this division, men adapted a stoic style, and women, an emotional one. But there are exceptions.

Within my own family, I am an emotional empath, as is one of my sons, Gabriel. Gabriel is as highly attuned to others' feelings as I am. You can only imagine our conversations.

"Mom, what's wrong?"

"Hmmm, nothing."

"That's not true. You're scared."

"You know, Gabe, I am. And I can tell that my fear is making you feel scared."

My other son has deep emotions but runs a different way. He relies on me to help him express his emotions. I still remember one conversation in which he was upset about something. My sentences were punctuated with statements like this.

"If I were you, I'd be really sad."

"Yes," he shared, his voice cracking.

"I'd also be mad that someone acted like that."

"I am!" he agreed.

I am intimate with both of my sons through my emotional empathy, but the relationships differ in that one son is more emotionally empathic and the other is empathic in other ways. The point is that we don't need to be in relationship with people exactly like us—we simply need to be able to use our gifts and for others to accept them.

Emotional empaths, in particular, must have their emotions accepted and validated, and they do best in relationships with people who can acknowledge their own emotions. Short of the latter, the emotional empath can easily become oversympathetic, taking on the other's emotions and acting them out. This is what is occurring any time you see one member of a couple histrionically expressing feelings while the other appears deadpan. Because of this tendency to carry all the emotional freight in a relationship, an emotional empath must use the steps to empathic compassion to separate their own emotions from another's and refuse to take in or act out feelings that are not their own.

Sometimes the emotional empath attracts friends or romantic companions who are anything but emotional, including individuals who manipulate others' emotions but can't relate to them inwardly. These people might display emotional contagion or narcissist-like traits, or be deeply depressed and unable to connect with their own emotions. An emotional empath can end up caring so much about these difficulties that they lose their own emotional compass in the process. On the upside, an emotional empath is wonderfully able to relate to impaired empaths such as those with ASD (autism spectrum disorder) or ADHD (attention deficit hyperactivity disorder), or even people who are depressed or anxious.

Mental Empathy: The Cheerleaders of the Universe

When it comes to figuring things out, such as what's really going on and what needs to be done, the mental empath takes the prize, hands down. Like a computer, a mental empath is able to sort through vast amounts of data pertaining to another and zero in on what's pertinent.

If you are a mental empath, you have much to contribute to a relationship partner. You know when your partner's spirit is flagging and how to help. You pinpoint the reasons behind low self-esteem or self-confidence and can zoom in on self-sabotaging beliefs. Better yet, you know which truths should be substituted for the lies that trigger those states. You know what actions will lead to success and which will head south. Likewise, you're a great parent or parental figure; you can unknot just about any problem and brainstorm a practical path forward.

The downsides of being a mental empath are twofold. First, you can end up feeling—or actually being—used. Because you can sense the underlying needs of others, they can turn to you for support and ignore the fact that you could use a return favor. You could also rely too much on your mental faculties, to the detriment of your own emotional or soul needs. You might end up using tools like imagination or hyperoptimism to fit in with someone who is emotionally based, or you may partner with an extremely emotional, physical, or shamanic sensitive to round out your personality. High mental empaths sometimes develop anxiety disorders because they can't shut off the flow of information; it can all become "too much." This might be the case with certain types of ADHD, which I believe could involve receiving so much intuitive mental data that it's hard to process explicit information too.

The beauty of mental empathy is the wisdom that gradually evolves with its appropriate use. Because of its link with clairaudience, a mental empath can become the interpreter of knowledge, the giver of truth, and the rational rock needed in just about any relationship.

Natural Empathy: Representing Mother and Father Nature

What can fill a natural empath with more love than connection with an animal, tree, or force of nature? Certainly natural empaths are able to bond with a mate, relatives, and friends, but they reserve a special place in their heart for the beings of nature they are uniquely attuned to.

I have one friend whose primary relationships are with her dogs. She has hosted several dogs over the years, often two at a time, and always seems to know exactly what they are thinking and feeling. Most of them live years longer than they are statistically supposed to, and I am sure it's because of her empathic care. In my own home, we have a guinea pig, Max, who is going on nine years old, more than twice the life expectancy for one of his kind. He lives in the dining room and can see everything that occurs from his perch. I believe he is the grand choreographer of many an activity in our household.

Natural empaths might relate to one particular type of natural being or nearly all of them, but they often find themselves speaking for their friends in nature. I once had a client come to my house for a session, and before she left, she handed me a notepad full of insights from my dogs, who had "spoken" with her during the session. The inaudible conversations were more like ransom notes, reading like this: *We'll leave you alone at five in the morning if you give us bones.*

Natural empaths are often able to share messages from the natural world with their human loved ones, and sometimes combine sensitivity to the plant and planetary worlds with a physically empathic healing ability. I once worked with a woman who could energetically tap into a client or a loved one and sense what type of star energy they needed. She could then feel which star in the sky could provide this unusual healing energy and send the starry light into the person in need. Yet other individuals, those who are often shamanically sensitive, are able to attune to foliage, trees, or even elements and then connect with the spirits of these forces, requesting that they send radiant healing empathy to another person.

In a romantic or family relationship, natural empaths often find themselves representing the natural world, instructing the people around them about how to better relate as well. They can be found putting stones under a child's bed or scolding a mate for killing a fly. This can present challenges for people who are not naturally sensitive and simply want to coexist with the element-loving empath rather than access the same sensitivity.

Spiritual Empathy: Knowing Best

"My wife doesn't always tell the truth," complained a husband. "Everyone else believes her, but I can always tell when she's lying. Of course," he added sarcastically, "she can do no wrong, and so I'm usually left feeling invalidated."

It turned out he was right and that the lying was more serious than fibbing on her taxes. About a year later, the husband discovered that his wife had been taking cash out of their account and gambling with it on business trips, during which time she was also conducting affairs. Her seemingly generous personality had alerted no one save him, primarily because he was a spiritual empath with the sixth sense needed to assess another's value system—or lack thereof.

In a relationship, you can't ask for a more decent partner than a spiritual empath. They simply can't live with themselves if they don't abide by their own value system. Whatever they profess as true, they will do their best to demonstrate. If they hold deep family values, they will be at every soccer game their child plays in. If they believe in fidelity, they won't stray even if their partner does. Unfortunately, the same sensitivity that allows them to gauge their own behavior against their beliefs also alerts them to others' fluctuating levels of self-responsibility and respectability.

For instance, I have a client who is married to a well-known lawyer and has to attend a lot of business events. She can't stand the events, mainly because she only has to sit near someone at a table or jostle their elbow around the punch bowl to know if they are deceitful or insincere. She simply senses it in her body. She is also endowed with the other spiritual empathic gift, which involves knowing another's true destiny. After one fundraiser, she said to her husband, "Do you think there are *any* lawyers who want to be lawyers rather than missionaries, dentists, authors, or something else?" Her spiritual powers are so intense, she can feel who is off-path and unhappy because of it.

If a spiritual empath is partnered with or in relationships with honest individuals, the relationships will flow smoothly. The challenge lies when other people are hiding something.

Ironically, spiritual empaths often attract at least one significant relationship with a less than savory individual in order to test their gifts and decide to believe in them. The mirror of a dishonest person also makes us look inside to expose parts of ourselves that are deceptive. Are we fooling ourselves, believing what we want to rather than what we should? Can we stop shaming ourselves and cease feeling unworthy of decent treatment?

Paradoxically, a spiritual empath is also highly susceptible to low self-esteem and therefore mistreatment in a relationship, simply because their standards are so high. There is a difference between being able to sense our spiritual possibilities and being able to live there. Ultimately, the best protection for a spiritual empath is grace—gracefulness and mercy for self, which can then be extended to others.

Because of their spiritual sensitivity, many spiritual empaths partner up with manipulative, impaired empaths who hide behind the "do-gooder" to look good themselves. They can also be kindly sensitive toward impaired empaths who struggle with issues caused by ASD, ADHD, depression, anxiety, or mental illnesses, including schizophrenia. A spiritual empath reads the purity of another's soul, not the way the person presents in the world. This characteristic is positive when the impaired empath is good-hearted but devastating when the impaired empath is narcissistic or manipulative and simply uses the spiritual empath for their own gain.

Some spiritual empaths are impaired themselves. They might be so attuned to the negativity in a family that they become depressed; they feel bad because they can't shift the family system. They might become bipolar in the sense of splitting their own so-called dark self from their light self, as they are unable to fully embrace the dark, or shadow, self that needs love and healing in order to evolve. I believe they can even develop the type of bipolar tendencies or schizophrenia that relates to a split soul. One part of them might be outside of the body, trying to help others, while the other part feels trapped inside the body.

Spiritual empaths are truly a light unto themselves and the world as long as grace takes the lead role in the play of their lives.

Shamanic Empathy: Here, There, and Everywhere

The shaman empath has entire worlds to draw companions from. This can either increase the propensity for love and joy in personal relationships or potentially detract from that experience.

As we have discussed, the pantheon of spiritual helpers includes natural beings, deceased relatives, spirit guides, and souls known in past lives. Ideally, all of these can support the shaman's close relationships. Besides bringing their own cornucopia of connections to the shaman empath in relationship, they are frequently able to tune in to helpers linked with the shaman's loved ones too.

This reservoir of assistants can bolster a relationship, with the invisibles serving as everything from matchmakers to parental advisors. Yet, as you might imagine, the large number of "insiders" can also become overwhelming and intrusive for the shaman and their loved ones alike.

I remember years ago spending all night awake in a hotel because I could sense the presence of visiting spirits. My husband wasn't too thrilled about the succession of others that paraded through the room and how that seized my energy and attention. Since then I've learned to screen out everyone and everything but the Divine, unless the Divine directs my focus to a visiting spirit or being, but it took years to accomplish that goal.

Shamanic empaths are gifted with at least partial access to all other empathic capabilities as well, making for yet another potential merry-go-round experience for them and their loved ones. The key ingredient for healthy relationships for the shamanic empath is boundaries; lacking these, the shaman can be plagued by nearly every relationship and empathic challenge. All the tools I presented in chapter 5 are of great help in establishing healthy boundaries.

Relationship Rx:
Applying the Five Steps
to Compassionate Empathy

How best to assure that your empathic gifts lead to successful and loving rather than challenging relationships? By appropriately applying the techniques for compassionate empathy. I suggest you practice these steps while thinking of a special relationship. Keeping your bond with a beloved other in mind, see what you can discover about it and your own gifts.

During this exercise—which you can conduct anytime you need to, whether you are with a loved one or not (and even if you don't like the person you most often empathize with)—I blend the questions related to each empathic style. We often find that when we open one paint tube or color of empathy, other abilities begin to arise. For this reason I am inviting your inner self to test for all forms of empathy. If you don't get a response to a certain style, simply ignore that area and continue.

Preparation: Conduct Spirit-to-Spirit

As before, affirm your inner spirit as well as that of your partner or close confidant, and then affirm the presence of the Greater Spirit.

STEP 1: *Ask for and Acknowledge Needed Information*

Concentrate on the relationship and ask the Divine to provide you with information about your role in it. What are you doing in it? What does it mean to you? What is it supposed to give to you—and what are you supposed to give to it? Now ask if there is a situation you need to zoom in on during this exercise and whether you can receive empathic understanding from the other person.

STEP 2: *Conduct Compassionate Assessment and Ask for Assistance*

Ask the Divine to provide deeper insight into the empathic information provided. Are there additional feelings your loved one has that you need to acknowledge? Are there mental perceptions that would help you better understand them? Is there a sense of their physical predicament or a being or force of nature that presents itself to provide information? Do you sense input directly from the Divine, get a sense of what is right or wrong with this person's current situation, or perceive something right or wrong with your relationship with them? Finally, is there insight from the otherworldly realms that compels your attention? You can also ask whether there are any clairvoyant or clairaudient messages you are supposed to receive.

Now focus on yourself for a moment. How do you feel about the information you've obtained? Does it stir an emotional or mental response inside you? Does your body feel comfortable or not? Have you in any way taken in the other's feelings, thoughts, or physical issues, not to register the data but in a way that will cause you problems by absorbing and holding it? If so, release these extra energies right now using a healing stream of grace to rebalance yourself.

Does it seem that the Divine wants you to continue in order to better understand the other's situation or your own relationship? Is there a right or wrong way to proceed? Do the entities or spirits that are present feel beneficial or harmful to your loved one, yourself, or the process? Are there any past-life or ancestral issues present—in you or your loved one—that might affect what is occurring? Follow divine input and use healing streams of grace if you need to perform any kind of protection or entity release or begin healing past traumas. Release yourself from the entire process if the Divine leads you to do that; otherwise, move ahead.

STEP 3: *Ask for a Divine Response*
Ask the Divine to provide healing for the other, for yourself, and for the relationship. Is there a part of you that wants to take over God's job and do the fixing for your loved one? Step back and let go.

STEP 4: *Take Action with Humility*
Are you called to serve? Then ask how. Are you supposed to do something for the other person, either on an initial or ongoing basis? Or is there perhaps something to stop doing? Conversely, is there something you need

them to do for you? Relationships are two-way streets, and we need to examine them from a variety of angles.

How about those emotions? Is there a way you could more significantly tend to the other's emotional well-being or ask for a return favor? Has there been discounting or a lack of validation on either side? If so, what might correct the situation?

Are there beliefs underpinning the relationship or either of your own individual roles in it that should be addressed and clarified, perhaps even changed? What is your job in this regard? Is there something to share with the other that will serve you both?

How might a tighter bond with nature assist the relationship? Do you collectively or individually need to spend more time outside or get a dog? Is there an insight or remedy that astrology or feng shui might provide? Are there natural forces that can be called upon? How about spiritual knowledge you should be aware of?

Along the same vein, ask what the ultimate purpose of the relationship is from the Divine's point of view. If it were to follow its highest destiny, what would the relationship become? What could happen in the future?

Now play "shaman therapist" for the relationship. What insights can be provided by examining past lives the two of you have experienced or the interplay between your souls? Are there past-life or soul issues you need to examine to support the relationship or your next step in (or out of) it? Is there an invisible "relationship counselor" that can come to your aid and, if so, what do they show you?

Finally, ask if there are any radiant empathy responses you might open to and offer for the other person, the relationship, or yourself.

STEP 5: *Surrender the Outcome*

No matter what you may have shifted in the preceding steps or not, ask the Divine to take charge from here on. Thank yourself, the other, and the Divine for this work.

Dealing with Difficult People

"Dear Abby" is the name of an advice column founded in 1956 by a woman under the pen name Abigail Van Buren. Through her column, she dispensed worldly wisdom and commonsense advice to generations of women and men. Her strong sense of healthy boundaries mixed with compassionate humor is what we need in spades when it comes to dealing with impaired empaths—as well as aspects of ourselves that might be impaired. (A reminder: for a detailed discussion of the varieties of impaired empaths, see appendix 2.)

The three techniques for compassionate empathy you have learned are vital when applied in a relationship. Still, challenging situations can arise that leave us feeling confused and distressed—until we learn a few tips for reclaiming our power. Some common scenarios are as follows.

Lost in a Crowd

Many empaths struggle to tune out others' energies when in a crowded place such as a school, shopping center, or party, or when standing on the street in a busy downtown area. The emotional empath might be flooded with others' feelings, and the mental empath "junked up" by others' thoughts, especially negative ones. The physical empath can easily feel compressed and sick, afflicted with everyone else's aches and pains, and the spiritual empath might start paying too much attention to this cacophonous ecosystem's striking challenges, which seemingly shouldn't exist. Shaman empaths might feel like they are literally exploding with the acute awareness of all the above, as well as the presence of both angelic and demonic forces and other entities.

The natural empath might pick up on the inorganic factors of a human-made environment and desire only to flee, struck with nausea or even a fever in reaction to its glues, paints, and power lines and other stressful EMF sources. They might sense the wounded nature of the one daisy growing out of a sidewalk or the wilting cries of the single plant attempting to grow in the corner of a mall.

A natural empath might also define a crowd differently from the other empaths. A crowd might be a logged forest replete with wounded tree trunks or a newly designed fracking site, the earth's shale bemoaning its fate. It might also be the reaction of the atmosphere to pollution or the fear of a flock of water birds faced with spilled oil.

Remember that your best empathic friend is Spirit-to-Spirit. Ask always for Spirit to filter and screen others' messages and energies for you, directing them away from your field when they are not beneficial. I like to visualize that the Divine places a great big blower fan in the front and back of me and sends these incoming energies upward to the heavens.

Also use your healing streams of grace, asking the Divine to surround you in layer upon layer of grace, which will filter others' energies so you only take in what serves the higher good. If necessary, get out of the environment. If you are in a class, sit near the door so you don't feel trapped. Find a bathroom and wash your hands, imagining that the water cleansing your hands is also clearing your energetic field. Concentrate on your most empathic chakra(s) and imagine a strong beam of color entering from the backside, the part of you that can open to heavenly energies. (For information on the meaning of colors, see page 134.) Call upon your spiritual guides and ask them to serve as sentries. You *can* be blissfully alone in a crowd, even if you don't think so.

Feeling Shut Down

As empathic as we might be at times, there are certain circumstances in which most of us shut down. I used to close off during family get-togethers and, consequently, left every holiday gathering with the flu or a cold, as my physical system wasn't able to clear out the incoming toxins. I also used to close off around narcissists, alcoholics, or people with bipolar disorder. My family was replete with individuals afflicted with these conditions, and my childhood self-protective mechanism was to imagine that I could crawl deep inside myself and shut the trapdoor behind me. The problem with this reaction was that despite the fact that I thought I was protecting myself from others' issues, I really wasn't; I still picked up on everything going on in them. Not only that, but I developed coping mechanisms that hurt me in relationships as an adult. How can you carry on a healthy adult-adult relationship if you close off when under pressure? Depending on your empathic style, you might shut down around animals in pain, thinking it's better to distance yourself than be unable to help, or turn off whenever you sense a ghost in the room, believing yourself indefensible to invisible intrusions.

How do you know you are shut down? Your body provides you with clues. You might become cold, which means you have shut your chakras and collapsed the energetic field around your skin. And unfortunately, the less electrical flow in your body, the more permeable your energetic boundaries. You might also experience a sudden flash of heat, which means you are allowing another's energy to flood you; heat indicates an influx of energy. If the heat is uncomfortable, you are allowing in energy you don't want, which in turn dampens your own energy and responsive intelligence.

A part of you might also numb out, which indicates that your conscious self has abandoned that part of your body. The danger in this is that others' energies can now enter. As well, you are now unable to connect with a necessary part of your body-mind-and-soul consortium to effectively problem-solve. You might also sense that you have separated from your body—that you are floating around outside yourself. This disconnection suggests that you have dissociated and that a part of your soul—and therefore your power—has fled your body. You could now easily be coerced and controlled by manipulative empaths or entities that wish to take advantage of the empty space your fear has left in its wake.

If you experience any of these signs, I suggest that you immediately stop whatever you are doing and conduct Spirit-to-Spirit, breathing deeply into your body until you feel that you have reconnected with yourself. You can then ask the Divine to fill you with healing streams of grace. If you are with someone, ask for a time out or a pause. If the other is asking you to do something, tell them that you will have to think about it. If you sense that you are being manipulated, you can simply say that something doesn't feel right and you need some time and space. Call a friend, go outside, take a walk, head to a yoga class, or do anything you need to do to integrate the part of you that has been triggered and has abandoned the rest of you. Then, when you have more time, perform the self-healing exercise on page 126 called "Self-Healing for Empaths."

Feeling Sorry for Others

How often do you descend into pity when you are around a hurting person or animal instead of remaining empathic? How often do you feel sorry for yourself instead of feeling empathic? It's easy to do, but it's not helpful to yourself or anyone else.

For example, I have a friend with a severely ADHD son. Samantha is a high emotional empath and easily attunes to Jared's frustration and hurt. Jared doesn't quite understand why he can't complete tasks at the same rate as his brother or why other kids sometimes stay away from him; ADHD kids often enter others' energetic spaces and make them uncomfortable. Samantha so deeply senses Jared's suffering that she excuses him from chores, does his homework for him, and tells him that his lack of friends is "their loss."

My youngest son is also extremely ADHD as well as dyslexic, but I refrain from pity. I actually perceive the condition as offering an inherent gift. Because Gabe has to try harder to do the same amount of schoolwork as other kids, he is extremely hard working. Instead of pitying him and compensating for his issues, I have had him work with an ADHD coach since he was four. I've had to learn how to set up rigid organization rules, which is very good for me, and monitor my own emotional reactions so I don't descend into pity.

Do I feel sorry for myself because I have to go the extra mile—or ten miles? I confess to feeling tired, but I also feel honored to be of service.

Instead of falling into the pity trap, we can use our empathy to look for the strengths in another and figure out what weaknesses we can strengthen inside ourselves. Learning how to be more patient and organized has done me—and the world—a world of good. I say this because these are two of the qualities that have enabled me to write books, lead workshops, teach classes, and counsel thousands of people.

A Relational Example: Narcissism in Others or Self

Let's examine one of the several types of impaired empaths to see how we can empathically relate to individuals with this disorder—and we may count ourselves in their number. I have selected the narcissistic condition because it is so widespread. The same concepts and techniques that help us relate to narcissists or our own inner narcissist can also be used with other overly self-focused individuals, including active addicts, individuals with bipolar disorder, and even people lost in depression and anxiety.

Narcissists are individuals who think mainly about themselves. Charming and bright, these people are actually empathic but are classically described as only mentally empathic. They simply don't understand—or care about—others' emotions.

The current standard of empathy only measures two basic types of empathy: mental and emotional. I believe that narcissists use their mental perceptions to manipulate others but can do the same with shamanic empathy, accessing darker forces to gain insight about another and using this information to get their needs met. I have also come across narcissists who can employ physical empathy, but mainly they use radiant empathy, sending their physical issues into others, primarily their romantic partners or children. (This is called "initiated compathy," as explained earlier in this chapter in the section on physical empathy.) Seldom do I find narcissists skilled in natural or spiritual empathy. A narcissist will believe that because they are human, the natural world is "beneath" them.

There are two main reasons a narcissist might not access their innate spiritual empathy. The first is that a spiritual being might see through the narcissist. Narcissists don't want anyone seeing their dirt, partly because they don't want to see it themselves. The second reason is that they want to be the most powerful or aware being in their personal universe. To acknowledge that a spiritual being operates at a higher level than they do is to feel like a failure or "lesser than."

Quite often, kind or highly empathic individuals are attracted into relationship with narcissists because the wounded child within the narcissist is calling out for help. Emotional empaths sense the agonizing abandonment issues and resulting hurt and pain underlying the narcissistic persona, while mental empaths perceive the crooked thinking processes. Both emotional and mental empaths long to fix or heal the infant or child locked inside the narcissist.

Physical empaths relate to the stuck state of the narcissist; energetically, narcissists are locked in the equivalent of a closet inside their bodies. Natural empaths become entranced if a narcissist can manipulate them through their companion animals, such as pretending to care about the animal, and spiritual empaths become enthralled by the prospect of "saving" narcissists, who are usually ethically off-path. Shamans fall prey if they are mesmerized and manipulated by the dark forces often accompanying the narcissist.

I have perceived—and best avoided—narcissists by paying attention to empathic clues, not my eyes. I feel emotionally scared around a narcissist. My mental empath twists my stomach when they are talking. My physical body gets cold and shuts down, and nature often sends disturbing signals to warn me. I decided not to date one man because after dreaming about him one night, everywhere I went there were police cars—hundreds of them. I figured I should avoid this person. For a short while I actually did date a narcissist, and when I was thinking of getting more serious, a tree in my yard was suddenly loaded with crows—hundreds of crows—that cawed at me every time I ruminated about this man. Recalling these experiences reminds me that our spiritual empathy tells us when others are lying and will help us catch them in their lies for the good of all concerned.

The shamanic world is most likely the richest mine for sensing and dealing with narcissists, those who can leave you feeling stripped of pride, worth, and even the resources they have conned out of you. Quite simply, narcissists cast spells.

The best way to deal with narcissists is to consider them enchanters who throw spells of glamour, first over themselves and then over you. They spin a seductive web and insert it into their energetic field to appear competent, attractive, and intelligent—which they might be. The thing is, narcissists can't stand to appear weak, ugly, or mistaken in any way.

When they smile or pay attention to you, they are using their physical radiant empathy to encode you with their desirability. Every empathic skill is spent reading you so as to find your hot buttons—not only to please you but also to shame you if you don't approve of them. Toward this end, they (usually unknowingly) enlist dark forces to support the manipulation—and vice versa. Narcissists are easily used by dark forces, which encourage them to hide their pain from the world as well as themselves. The dark forces thereby keep them enthralled and unable to achieve their higher purpose.

By paying attention to your empathic clues, you can spot a narcissist and use the three main techniques: Spirit-to-Spirit, healing streams of grace, and five steps to compassionate empathy. I find the most gentle and appropriate way to break the spell, to push away the enchantment, is to send healing streams of grace toward the infant or young child locked inside of the narcissist. They might not immediately decide to face their deeper issues, but you will dismiss the codependent aspect of you that longs to heal those in need. By using the healing streams of grace, you let go and let God.

But what if *you* are a narcissist? Well, as I touched on earlier, the truth is that we all have at least a narcissistic wound, a psychological injury inflicted upon us when we were young. In the context of intuitive empathy, these wounds can also be carried in from past lives or be triggered through our epigenes. They can also result in a splintered soul and vulnerability to entity interference.

These wounds, which might or might not result in a full-blown narcissistic personality disorder, are caused by our parents' inability to meet our emotional needs when we were growing up. The result is a sense of emptiness and disconnection, which we try to fill through grandiosity and perfectionism, as well as by projecting our issues upon others. The part of us that feels constantly maligned or better than others might be inflicted with a narcissistic wound. If we fall prey to believing ourselves a martyr or a victim, we might be dealing with our inner narcissist. As well, if we are constantly attracting narcissists into our life, it might serve us to figure out whether we have a narcissistically wounded self that attempts to feel good—and even better than others—by trying to continually fix others.

We don't want to reject our narcissistic self, but neither do we want to put this injured self in charge of our relationships. Instead, I recommend devoting time to conducting the self-healing exercise in chapter 6. Then pay attention to indications that you may be lost in or acting out of your narcissistic self, which could include feeling a lot of self-pity, the sense of being continually put down or unimportant, the desire to blame others, or the need to take over a situation because "no one else can get it right." You can also take yourself through the "An Example of Healing" exercise in chapter 6 to examine your own PTSD conditions.

Know that you can also use your dream life for diagnosis and healing work. Before going to bed, ask for a dream that will help you perceive your wounded child. Every time you wake, write down the dream or the lingering feeling from an unremembered dream. You can do this for several nights. When you sense you understand the traumas that created your abandoned self, begin asking for healing when you go to sleep. Keep track of these dreams as well. Continue this exercise until you have a sense of further healing work you might need to do.

Opening to Empathic Understandings

Are you struggling to understand something or someone? I will close this chapter with a simple exercise you can try to open your empathy.

1. Conduct Spirit-to-Spirit.

2. Sit comfortably and breathe deeply into your heart. Now concentrate on the person or being you want to empathize with.

3. Allow your mind to free-associate with all feelings, thoughts, awareness, perceptions, and even words, tones, colors, shapes, symbols, and images that arise. (Know that you can also hold an object related to this person, especially if you are highly physically empathic.)

4. Refrain from deciphering which associations come from empathy rather than your mind. Simply continue with the process until every awareness narrows down to a single knowing and the feeling of compassion.

5. Concentrate on this distilled information and ask the Divine to provide you further understanding of its meaning and what you should do with this knowledge.

6. Sending healing streams of grace to the other and return to your normal state.

At the most fundamental level, understanding your empathic gifts in relationships is the basis for understanding your empathic gifts, period. The seeds of empathy are sown within in order to grow into vines of connection without. Paradoxically, by analyzing the ways we interact with others—physically, emotionally, mentally, naturally, spiritually, and shamanically—we inevitably come more "into ourselves," into our compassionate heart. We fulfill the prerequisite for knowing best how to fulfill our calling to care.

CHAPTER 8

Empathy and Your Vocation: The Calling to Care

*Power comes not from the barrel of a gun, but from
one's awareness of his or her own cultural strength
and the unlimited capacity to empathize with, feel
for, care, and love one's brothers and sisters.*

ADDISON GAYLE, JR.

Empathy links us so we can care for each other, and how better to accomplish this great goal than within the circle of compassion that we call "work"?

Take a moment to consider your own relationship with work. Even as a child, you felt compelled toward greatness. You knew that you were here to make a difference, largely through your work—which, when it reflects your spirit and spiritual gifts, is called a vocation or calling.

Maybe you are living your calling, or perhaps you are still searching the stars for that unique purpose. Perhaps you've been operating on this highest of levels already and didn't even know it, writing it off as "just parenting" or "making a living at a *job* job." The truth is that if you are employing your empathic and other intuitive gifts, you are living your destiny. There might be more gems to uncover, other careers to explore, new roads to walk, but you are on-purpose. Increased understanding of your empathic gifts and greater skillfulness with them can only further enhance your vocation.

One of the unexpected pearls related to empathy is that understanding your empathic style can actually help you figure out your all-important calling. Want a clue about your calling? Well, it will have to incorporate your spiritual gifts.

In this chapter, we're going to explore the various applications of empathy at work, showcasing each style, one at a time. We'll emphasize ways you can use each style to bolster your work success and look at examples of these empathic styles in the working world. We'll then cover a few tips on how to best access and apply the three main techniques for compassionate empathy in this context. Finally, I'll share a few ways you can use but also disguise your empathy in workplaces that aren't amenable.

Know that this information applies whether you are paid for a living or not, whether you work for someone else or for yourself. Your vocation isn't dependent on money but on following the call of your soul.

Empathy at Work

How does your empathy look and function at work? The following descriptions will help you better understand and use these vital gifts.

Physical Empaths: The Solid Super-Person

Have you ever watched a Superman movie or show? Superman and his marvelous superhero companions are physical empaths, hard at work saving humanity from itself. Extraordinarily physical, they can literally move matter to do what matters. (Needless to say, as superheroes they have other finely honed skills as well.)

If you're a physical empath, your physical body is not only your human uniform but also your soul's traveling vehicle. It will register anything and everything that you are called to know, feel, or fix in this mechanical universe.

Physical empaths can end up in any profession, even parenting and homemaking, but they are always dedicated to providing materially for others in one way or another. They often walk this earth as healers, as they are so attuned to others' physical maladies. Many also make their way into the financial sector because they know that money is anything but optional on this planet. Of course, they could also be football players or coaches, jewelers or clothiers, but whatever their job description, they are devoted to enhancing others' physical existence.

As has been clear throughout this book, physical empaths must guard their health, avoiding the tendency to take on responsibilities that are not theirs to carry. Avoid giving yourself away; save some of that money for yourself. Conversely, avoid gluttony and greed. Your commitment to physicality can lead to obsessiveness if you don't prioritize balance in your life. Remember to support your physical self by paying attention to your mind, emotions, and spirit.

Emotional Empaths: Feelings, Anyone?

Decades ago, I started in my first corporate job. One of the female vice presidents took me aside and said, "There is only one rule: no emotions. Ever. If you are going to cry, do it at home."

An emotional empath might believe they should just pack their bags and stay at home if that's the attitude in their workplace. You can no more stop sensing others' feelings than you can desist from feeling your own. Fortunately, this gift is ideal for a variety of professions, even if you are rooted in a corporate environment.

Emotional empaths excel in tasks that require kindness, mercy, compassion, care, and the human touch. Many therapists, training professionals, parents, social workers, human resource experts, and creatives are emotional empaths. You don't need to confine yourself to the so-called helping professions or creative arts, however. I have an emotionally empathic client who is an accountant, but not in the typical spreadsheet sense. She hires and places people for her company's accounting teams because she has a knack for sensing who would be happy at which jobs.

Of course, the emotional empath has to be careful not to get emotionally used up at work. Sensing everyone's feelings is exhausting, and it's easy to become overextended. Make sure you balance your emotional receptivity with the opposite, including plenty of exercise, fun, alone time, and time spent with people who listen to you, not only the other way around.

Mental Empaths: Organizing Another's Canvas of Dreams

Knowledge-based mental empaths are valuable assets in the world of work, as they can easily distinguish what is occurring from what should be occurring. They also know how to problem-solve to close the gap. Able to easily read people, especially their motivations, they can create systems out of a weaving of intuitive information and logical data, both meeting specific objectives and attaining higher goals.

Mental empaths are brilliant in professions that require research, project management, analytical skills, problem solving, reasoning, and motivating others. They are excellent at working in for-profit or nonprofit organizations that require these and other skills. Their organizational abilities also lend themselves to making wise financial investments or running a business in a logical fashion.

If you are a mental empath, watch out for people and systems that rely on your abilities and forget to give you credit. Some might prefer to throw mud at you instead of bettering their own performance. Know, too, that some people might not like you, seeing you as too picky or analytical.

Natural Empaths: Get Thee Outside— or Bring Outside Inside

Natural empaths let their love of nature serve as a trusted guide, seeking always to represent their fellow natural and celestial companions. Their attunement to sensing what natural beings and forces are going through is often accompanied by shamanic instincts and the ability to link with the spirit-based natural energies as well as the physical, emotional, mental, and spiritual sensations their connections are experiencing.

Natural empaths are always happier working outside or bringing a little more of the outside into human-made places and spaces. Plant-oriented empaths might work as gardeners, landscapers, forest rangers, or agriculturists; animal lovers could be vets, dog walkers, bird watchers, or fishery specialists. Naturalists oriented toward physical healing could become herbalists, naturopaths, or organic chefs, and those with a strong dose of emotional empathy might become psychic animal communicators or dolphin trainers. Naturalists with visual capabilities could become green builders, interior designers, or feng shui masters. There are hundreds of different types of jobs for a natural empath.

As we've discussed throughout this book, it's important that a natural empath establish correct boundaries—the five steps to compassionate empathy is an excellent method—so they do not lose themselves in their love of nature. As well, a natural empath can be especially sensitive to the variety of inorganic substances and EMFs found in work environments, often including noxious chemicals, artificial lighting, and buzzing computers and electrical lines. I recommend that you use some of the amulets made to deflect EMFs; those made by BioGeometry are especially useful. (See the Vesica Institute site for medallions, listed in the jewelry section of their online store.[46]) Also, remember that people are natural beings too; each one of us is deserving of love and service.

Spiritual Empaths: Making Ethics Top Priority

The kit bag of a spiritual empath includes some of the most important of divine qualities: values, ethics, mission, morality, consciousness, and goodness. These factors are facets of love that bring heaven a little closer to earth.

Spiritual empaths can fill any type of job but often fill the role, if not the title, of priest, coach, pastor, rabbi, or spiritual counselor among their fellow human beings. You are the person who senses whether others are fulfilling their destiny or not, acting with integrity or not. You are the person who also senses negative agendas and lies.

If you have a shamanic bent, you might also attune to the presence of angelic or demonic forces and be aware of their effects on individuals. I know many spiritual empaths who have ended up as addiction counselors, essentially exorcising the dark forces that are steering their clients wrongly, or therapists doing the same for their patients.

Be careful not to believe that another's evil, malignant, manipulative, or immature choices are your fault. The fact that you sense truth doesn't mean you are in charge of teaching others to follow it.

Shamanic Empaths: One Person, Many Worlds

Shamanic empaths often struggle to find their place in the Western world because there are few places in it for someone with so many sensitivities. While in the indigenous world, they can openly call themselves shamans or priest-healers and do everything their gifts enable them to do; in the contemporary world, however, they must often disguise themselves behind one or several of their gifts.

For instance, a shamanic empath excelling in physical empathy might become a holistic doctor or chiropractor; a shaman with a strong emotional orientation could work as a therapist who performs regressions for current or past lives. A shaman with a leaning toward mental empathy might become a transformational life coach, while those inclined toward natural empathy could lead group treks to Machu Picchu and other natural wonders or enjoy life as organic farmers. The shaman empath who has a strong relationship with spiritual empathy can excel at helping people remove entities and cords (energetic connections to other beings) or make the great transition through death into the afterlife.

If you are a shamanic empath, know that you deserve to have your own life. You are not only here to serve the living and the dead, the worldly and the otherworldly; your life counts too. The help you provide to others? Partake of some of it yourself.

Applying the Five Steps to Compassionate Empathy at Work

At work (or even play), the three techniques I introduced in chapter 5, including the five steps to compassionate empathy, assure you proper energetic boundaries, guaranteeing you the space and breathing room required to make sure you don't fall into any of the empathic traps such as overextending, sympathizing, or being manipulated. Following is a synopsis of these steps as they apply to issues of work and finances.

When you are dealing with purpose-related issues, I recommend that you ask the Divine to work through your gifts to provide insights.

Preparation: Conduct Spirit-to-Spirit

STEP 1: *Ask for and Acknowledge Needed Information*

Focus on the work situation at hand. You might be thinking about a project, concentrating on a financial issue, or sitting in a meeting. You could be strategizing your future career or determining your ultimate spiritual mission. What empathically delivered information do you need directly from the Divine to steer you right or provide necessary insights? Spend a few moments making sure you are also pinpointing the exact goal the Divine wants you to focus on.

STEP 2: *Conduct Compassionate Assessment and Ask for Assistance*

You now want to remain open to the stream of empathic information you need to better understand the nature of your question and related insights, advice, or information. Sometimes we're shown situations from the past as a way to explain how we got into a tough situation—why our job doesn't suit us, why we are confused, why our money issues are strangling us. If you sense that you need to acknowledge past or present errors, start by receiving compassion from the Divine, and make sure to apply the same to yourself.

STEP 3: *Ask for a Divine Response*

It is time to step aside and allow the Divine to move unimpeded. Clear your mind and ask the Divine for direct advice about your purpose or specific issues related to it. Purpose-related information is ultimately about our life mission, the reason we came to this planet as embodied spirits. It is the calling that makes our hearts beat and our souls sing. Our purpose encompasses not only our soul lessons—the sometimes "hard knocks" experiences that stretch us to love when we'd rather not—but also activates the spiritual perfection that we've already achieved underneath the human mask we wear.

While asking for the Divine's responses, know that the sky is the limit. You can request radiant empathy; you can ask for insights. Always available are healing streams of grace, which can carry anything from inspiration to opportunities your way. It can also be helpful to request that the Divine open the path to the future, moving away obstructions and blocks. When you feel complete with step 3, it can also be helpful to ask the Divine what role it will continue to play as you move forward. This way you are assured of constant contact.

STEP 4: *Take Action with Humility*

This step might involve any number of activities. It could include several action steps such as checking the Web for jobs or writing a résumé.

It might involve an attitude shift such as starting to believe in yourself. It might also include using your radiant empathy gifts and sending energy to others, to a situation, or even into a vision or goal the Divine asks you to hold for your future.

This step can actually continue long after you meditatively commence it. Taking action toward purpose is an ongoing process, one with no clear walls or parameters. After all, when are you *not* "on-purpose"? Is your spirit off-duty after you've punched the clock and headed home for the day? Are you any less your essence simply because you are sleeping or making breakfast?

For instance, a spiritual action could involve asking for a dream that could assist you in making a work decision. It could include baring your soul to a friend, sharing childhood wounds in order to be clear about patterns that need to change. Because spiritual purpose is about your spirit, which is the totality of yourself, almost anything in your life can be labeled a purpose-driven activity. As you can imagine, however, this kind of thinking can also be a setup for workaholism, the loss of balance in the drive for success. One of the reasons I propose that you devote yourself consciously to asking the Divine to show you what actions to take is to refrain from overactivity. By paying attention to what the Divine and your own guidance suggest as important activities, you indirectly release yourself from doing other things.

After taking the actions you first feel directed toward, also ask to keep receiving signs and omens as you move forward. The Divine can continue to share with you through your emotions and perceptions, or perhaps by literally maneuvering your physical environment or body into certain activities. Natural beings might show up to assist you, or your own sense of right and wrong or a conviction of goodness might show you what to do (or not do). Shamans might receive dreams, visitations from invisible beings, and more. Stay in touch with the Divine to remain in touch with yourself.

STEP 5: *Surrender the Outcome*

We never really know what the Divine has in store for us or what others might choose to do or not do. Life is a journey, a blessing, and a continual unfolding of the unknown into the known—and work is that same kind of ever-unfolding blessing. Embrace each opportunity and occurrence, and remember that the Divine is with you.

Disguising Empathy at Work

As much as I wish I didn't have to say this, you might sometimes need to disguise your empathic abilities and responses at work. I wonder how many CEOs could get by with a statement like "I feel like you are sad" or which accountants can directly state "I know you're lying." There are ways in which each empathic type can reveal their empathic insights and still come across as businesslike with bosses, coworkers, employees, vendors, or other work contacts.

For instance, an emotional empath can use body language to address a workmate's emotions. People trust those who mimic their facial affects or body states, while compassion is implied by adding features that show you care. Blend these two sensory communications to genuinely support another.

Do you sense someone is sad? Slightly tilt your lips down while leaning forward as if to provide comfort. Is someone angry? Pucker your forehead but shift backward in a vulnerable position, validating the other's anger but opening your heart to emphasize that you are not afraid.

You can also use language that indicates sensitivity to the other without directly stating their emotions. If the other person is scared, you can package your affirmative validation by saying something like "this research project is scary" or "wow, I got nervous that I was late."

Mental empaths can easily bolster others' egos or performance by using uplifting statements that contain positive beliefs to cancel out their negative ones. A simple comment like "your project is a valuable contribution" can disengage another from their feelings of inadequacy.

You can also employ calming techniques if the other person is trapped in anxiety or a poor self-image. Many a mental empath assists other individuals or a team by leading people step by step into a more optimistic outlook or set of activities. For instance, you can say something like this: "How about if we first examine the numbers and then see what they mean?" Creating a logical framework allows others to do good work and expand into their best selves.

Physical empaths, like emotional empaths, can also use body language and employ props to creatively assuage others' issues or fears. One of the most successful female executives I have ever met confessed to me that she could sense all her employees' issues in her body. She couldn't exactly make comments like "Bob, your aching shoulder is stopping you from focusing at work" or "Jamie, I sure wish you'd deal with your alcohol addiction." Instead, she used the environment to help her.

The executive filled her office with knickknacks, as well as a variety of coffees, teas, and food items. She might hand Bob a small stone, one that energetically heals body pain, and laughingly tell him the stone asked to spend the day on his desk. She might serve tea to Jamie during meetings until Jamie finally confides in her, and she can then set Jamie up with a treatment center. Physical empaths, as this CEO demonstrated, can always use their ecosystem to do their work for them.

Natural empaths often work with beings or forces of nature, even if they are not formally paid for their efforts. Their greatest challenges, as we've seen throughout this book, are oversensitivity because of a high affinity to feeling the suffering that happens in nature and reactivity to artificial substances or energies.

The secret to surviving as a natural empath in a polluted world is to access natural assistance. For instance, imagine you're a forest ranger who feels the pain of all woodland creatures. You might link to the living spirit of a star to send healing energy to wounded animals. You might carry specific stones such as pink quartz, which emanates love, to remind yourself that the Divine has it all handled and you don't need to feel guilty for what you can't control.

Let's say that EMFs strip your energetic boundaries of their ability to protectively buffer you. You might slip a little pink flannel square in your pocket; pink flannel absorbs EMFs. Wash the flannel patch every day and reuse it. You could also wear rubber-soled shoes, which keep you grounded and send negative energies into the ground, and fill your office with plants and stones.

Are you a spiritual empath? It can be difficult to represent right from wrong when almost no one else does. Equally problematic is your ability to determine who is on-purpose and who is not. If you want to use your gift and still remain popular, refrain from telling anyone that they are a liar, hypocrite, embezzler, or thief. It's far better to use positive suggestions such as "I know you want to do the right thing, so how about if we do this?" or "Let's use our ethics as our guide and try it this way."

Because of your spiritual sensitivity, I recommend that you eventually make your way into a company or business that represents your core values. Businesses often need ethical project managers, coaches, team leaders, and other visionaries. Be who you are, and the rest will happen.

Shamans stand out in a normal business like a cactus in a rose garden. They are often seen as prickly, oppositional, or unusual, so make this work for you. Become the "go to" person for problem solving and truly thinking outside the box. Without making yourself sound weird, infer that you have a strong intuition and offer just enough meaningful input that people start to believe in you. Find the people in your office who are interested in the same type of invisible things that you are and form an alliance, supporting each other in the subtle exploration and application of your gifts. Know, too, that you might work best alone, almost like an undercover consultant. After all, you know you're not really alone—there is a world of a thousand angels there to help.

CONCLUSION

Embrace Your Gifts: The Joy of Empathy

To touch the soul of another human being is to walk on holy ground.

STEPHEN COVEY

Every time I read the last page of a book, I feel like I've ended a journey. My vacation, work trip, odyssey, or voyage is over, and now I take stock before I return home. Are there gifts to share? Did I *really* buy that wild outfit I'll never wear again? Do I carry souvenirs that will remind me of my time away?

Regardless of whether or not I can still close my suitcase, the best excursions are those that leave me changed, my soul touched in ways that hint of transformation. This is the mark of a successful journey. This is what occurs when we have learned and grown, not only shopped and toured. When this is the case, even the idea of "home" takes on a different meaning. It becomes more than where we live, whether this "where" is our physical abode or our bodily temple. It becomes the way in which we express the immortal spirit that houses what really counts: goodness, faith, truth, and, of course, love.

My sincerest wish is that, although our time together is drawing to a close, your own empathic journey is far from over. After you turn the last page of this book, I hope you will retain a new, deeper, and expanded awareness of what empathy is, how it works, and the myriad ways it manifests. More importantly, I hope these understandings now belong to you—that they no longer remain locked in the words but become embodied within you. If this has occurred for you, the questions you'll want to ask yourself include the following:

- What will I do with my increased understanding?
- How will I put these spiritual gifts to work to enrich my own life and that of others?

With a solid foundation in the empathic gifts, you now know that empathy is a gem with many facets. You have no doubt seen yourself in some of these pages as you have discovered its physical, emotional, mental, natural, spiritual, and shamanic aspects. You have had many opportunities to consider where your own empathic strengths lie and which areas you might like to further develop. You have become familiar with the qualities that masquerade as empathy but, in fact, serve to undermine it; you are learning to discern the difference. You know that there is empathy that only involves receiving and empathy you can radiate out to others—and that all empathy takes place at the energetic subtle-body level.

You know that there is a thing called impaired empathy and have had a chance to think about some common mental and emotional challenges in this new light. You may have had difficulty or confusion related to empathy in the past. Whether this is true for you or not, you now have tried-and-true tools to guide and protect you from this point forward, all safely tucked inside your empathy medicine bag—or maybe it's your "shopping bag," full of items for a new wardrobe, additional ways to show yourself to the world.

The full power of empathy belongs to you now. I have placed the keys in your hands with pleasure. When you embrace the empathic gifts, you become a living, breathing antidote to our society's empathy deficit disorder starting now, on this day. You are a counterweight to the widespread narcissism of our age. And this means that whether or not you decide to use your empathic gifts to engage the role of empathic healer, you are nonetheless a healing force in this world simply by means of your conscious presence.

The most powerful journeys are never over. If you are empathic—and if you have read this book, you are—what remains is to embrace your empathic gifts with joy as you continue this voyage called life. Please do not be concerned with the destination. It is the pathway itself that is your true birthright: *connection*—the very fabric of love.

APPENDIX 1

Sympathy (and Other Empathy Impostors)

When someone really hears you without passing judgment
on you, without trying to take responsibility for you,
without trying to mold you, it feels damn good...

CARL ROGERS

We all love to be heard and seen. We like the warmth that accompanies being understood and cared about. That's empathy at work. But sometimes what we experience from others or engage in ourselves isn't really empathy. It's a substitute for empathy, and it doesn't feel very good, especially when we're the ones who are being sympathetic instead of empathetic.

As I first explained in chapter 3, you are sympathetic rather than empathetic when you experience too much—when it becomes hard to separate your own experiences from what's happening to others. If you find yourself wondering why you are frequently (maybe even constantly) overwhelmed with sensations, feelings, knowings, spirits, and heightened awareness, you are probably experiencing sympathy rather than empathy.

In this section of the book, we are going to further explore the distinctions between sympathy and empathy, drawing on an example before defining the differences between the two. We'll also delve into the various symptoms you might experience if you are too sympathetic, and then outline the connections between sympathy and its cunning cohorts: personalizing, imagination, pity, emotional contagion, and hyperoptimism. Finally, we'll discuss the various ways in which being too sympathetic can adversely affect you when you're using your gifts for radiant empathy (see chapter 4).

As you read through this section, keep track of the different ways you might lean toward sympathy instead of empathy. Refer back to part II for ideas and techniques to help you remain whole and healthy during a variety of life experiences that have a tendency to elicit sympathy. To enjoy your empathic gifts and be of compassionate service with them is to stop being sympathetic and commit solely to being empathic.

The Sympathetic Empath

Janice sat on the couch in front of me, crying. She was stricken with so many problems that I didn't know where to start.

"My body aches all the time, so badly I want to cry," Janice related, twisting her hands in pain. "But that's not the only reason I'm sad. I'm simply depressed, and meds and therapy haven't worked."

I asked what she felt like when she wasn't sad.

She looked at me, puzzled. "I don't know," she answered. "I'm truly always sad."

Janice continued to describe her life.

"I'm disliked at work because I know more than the other secretaries, and they don't like it. Worse, I can also figure out if people are lying, which ruins most of my personal relationships. So I go outside to calm myself down and end up feeling even worse. I mean, how can people walk outside when the animals are so sad these days? And when the plants are being smothered by pollution?"

Just when I thought Janice's life couldn't sound more stressful, she added the following:

"But the real reason I came to you is that I sense things."

"Things?" I probed.

"You know. You're intuitive," she said. "Things like—those things that go bump in the night."

As an intuitive consultant, I am well acquainted with all things mystical, including spooks, ghosts, guides, déjà vu, signs, omens, and predictions about the future. The most wide-ranging of empathic gifts, shamanic empathy, includes being able to sense what is occurring in the spirit world. I needed to determine the exact relationship between Janice and the otherworldly realms.

"What happens to you when you sense spirits or you feel them contacting you?" I asked.

"When am I not?" Janice asked, starting to cry again. "All I have to do is walk in a room and I can sense who was most recently in there. I can also feel all their guides and angels, but not only the good ones—also the bad ones. In fact, I think that sometimes the bad entities actually come into me, and I can't get them out. You have to help me. I am overwhelmed."

As I worked with Janice, it became obvious that she was a shamanic empath, meaning she was able to receive information that was physical, emotional, mental, natural, and spiritual, in addition to otherworldly. Her problem wasn't a lack of empathic gifts, it was that her gifts were working against her rather than for her. In fact, her beautiful and instinctive empathy was creating muddle after muddle. Because she didn't yet understand how to manage her gifts, patterns were set in motion that resulted in some of the other "deadly substitutes" for empathy such as pity for others and naivety in selecting relationships.

We'll return to Janice and how she was able to help herself, with a little help from myself and others, after more closely examining this issue of sympathy versus empathy.

Sympathy versus Empathy:
Holding Instead of Registering

Empathy is the ability to mutually experience what is occurring in people, beings, forces, or objects outside the self. Besides being an ingrained survival capability, it is a spiritual gift. It enables us to stretch outside our own skin and, for a moment, become something we are not. If we feel called, we can compassionately respond to others' needs, easing their pain and suffering and maybe even dancing with them in their joy on occasion. In the end, this process invites us to become more than we've ever been.

In our culture, we sometimes use the word *sympathy* to describe the experience of empathy, but the two are very different. Sympathy can be a potentially wounding, if not dangerous, way of interacting with ethereal and intangible information, often causing a loss of self, health, and personal integrity or wholeness. Empathy, by contrast, carries none of these perils.

At the most basic level, sympathy is *holding* another's energy while empathy involves *registering* another's energy. Think of the difference between these two ways of interacting in this way:

Imagine that I approach you with a huge tub of bills, invoices, and tax notices, all of which I've been collecting for ten years. I've paid a few of them, but I've been so overwhelmed, I finally started throwing all my troublesome financial paperwork in a big container. It's pretty obvious that I don't want to deal with these bills, so I ask you to take the tub from me.

What are you going to do?

If you are sympathetic, you'll say yes. I will hand you the container, and even though I see you struggling with it, I figure it's your problem now. After all, you said yes.

If you are empathic, you'll look at me with concern and say, "Wow, that's a pretty big load. I can sense how overwhelmed you are."

If you sense that you are spiritually called to be compassionate or altruistic, you might ask if I want a hand going through the bills or if I need the name of a good tax person. In other words, you register or acknowledge what I'm going through, but you don't actually pick up a load that belongs to me and take it from me.

What might Janice's life look like if she were less sympathetic and more empathetic? She actually experienced the following changes as she learned to register external information rather than hold on to it. Notice that because Janice is a shamanic empath, these changes encompass all six categories of empathy.

PHYSICALLY: Better health. Janice's aches and pains gradually went away once she realized that she was taking on others' inflammatory issues and illnesses. She had started this sympathetic interaction with her mother when she was a child, unconsciously deciding that her mother might be more loving if she, Janice, carried her physical discomforts, which were many. Janice ultimately had to decide that she was lovable as she was and didn't need to earn value by taking on others' illnesses and physical pain. (Once Janice took the next few steps, she was inspired to eat healthier food as well, which also decreased the inflammation in her body.)

EMOTIONALLY: Less sadness and more joy. Janice had established an unconscious agreement with her father, a sorrowful alcoholic. As a small child, Janice had unconsciously believed she could "fix" her father by absorbing and holding his sadness. She had energetically continued this pattern by sympathetically absorbing others' sadness everywhere she went. While she might have first empathized with her father out of love, she had only injured herself—and not helped her father—by becoming sympathetic rather than simply empathetic.

MENTALLY: Making more friends. Janice was perceived as a "know it all" at work because she was receiving mental information all the time—and then sharing it. There's nothing wrong with being smart. Mentally empathic people often use their perceptions to brilliantly solve problems, manage projects, offer motivational talks, and compose creative solutions. The issue was that Janice was picking up on data that wasn't necessary for her own job performance and, without meaning to, lording her knowledge over others. As we worked together, she learned how to screen this information so she only tuned in to the mental energy that would support her and, secondarily, others. After Janice had strengthened her mental boundaries for a few months, her work mates found her more likable, and she could actually count a couple of them as friends.

NATURALLY: Love of being outdoors. Being a natural empath can be a hard row to hoe for someone as extremely gifted as Janice, someone who couldn't even walk in a garden without attuning to the flowers still smarting from having their blossoms picked. As Janice learned to consciously block unnecessary senses using the tools already covered in this book, she started to enjoy nature again. Her stress level dropped significantly when she was again able to take long walks in the local park.

SPIRITUALLY: Acceptance of others. Janice's instinctual ability to empathically sense when others were being dishonest was creating a judgmental attitude in her, and people reacted to this. Without knowing it, she was making a mistake many sympathetic people make: she believed herself responsible for others' spiritual and ethical issues. After our work, Janice was able to leave well enough alone and concentrate on her own integrity. As she shifted, she found that other people naturally began to share with her their deeper questions about their life purpose and the overall meaning of life. Her empathic spiritual gift now prompted others to trust her with their deepest concerns, and she was able to truly be of service.

SHAMANICALLY: Freedom from otherworldly interference. Most of us like to receive revelations and insights from divine sources. Personally, I believe that at least 90 percent of our world is invisible, composed of beings, forces, and energies that we can only touch with the clairs and empathic gifts. But not all that populates the supernatural world is good. As I sometimes share when I'm teaching, the fact that a dead person is dead (and serving time as a ghost or guide) doesn't mean that they know any more than the living.

Janice was way too exposed to the murkier side of the supernatural, to beings that had no business being involved in her life. When otherworldly forces intervene to the point that we are adversely affected, we call them *interference,* a word that clearly describes what they are doing. Janice's level of shamanic sympathy had reached gargantuan proportions, as indicated by the fact that spirits entered and occupied her body.

From the point of view of spiritual principles, this activity is clearly off-limits. Our bodies are our own; they are not meant to be used by others, whether they are living or deceased. It took time, but Janice eventually learned that she could stop spirits from possessing or occupying her, and she put a limit on her exposure to knowledge that didn't serve her, such as information about the long dead who had once occupied a house.

As time went on, Janice actually started to employ and enjoy her shamanic empathy. She decided to hone it into the ability to receive nightly dreams that could assist her and others. Eventually, she started a small side business as a dream interpreter, which earns her extra money and provides her pleasure.

To help Janice achieve these great strides, I used the basic tools I described to you in chapter 5. The first step I took, however, was to help her decide that she didn't need to use her empathic gifts to sympathize or hold on to others' energies; rather, she could find a path that would enable a loving exploration and use of her empathic gifts, an exploration that would support her own life rather than set her up to react to others.

What Does Sympathy Look Like?

There are many symptoms that can indicate that we are sympathizing instead of empathizing. If they occur commonly or often around a certain person, group, or situation, the general signs include the following:

- feeling overwhelmed or overtaken
- a sense of confusion: of being fused with something or someone else in a way that leads to disorientation or a lack of clarity
- loss of energy, exhaustion, or fatigue
- being plagued with diseases, feelings, thoughts, beliefs, sensations, and dreams or by forces or entities that you can't get rid of
- the sense that you can't control what happens to you
- a sense of guilt if you are unable to assist or help others
- physical pains occurring where you take on others' energies

These symptoms are only a few that describe what can occur if you sympathize rather than empathize. The following list of the differences between sympathy and empathy can further strengthen your discernment skills.

	Sympathy	Empathy
Overall:	Takes on the energies of others, absorbing them into the self	Senses the energy of others and consciously registers what is being transmitted
	Another's energy is absorbed into the self	Registers another's energy
	Displaces or injures own energy	Enhances own energy
	Relieves or excuses others from taking responsibility	Enhances others' sense of responsibility
	Causes confusion by fusing with another	Creates more clarity for self and other
	Can stimulate care that turns to concern and overwhelm	Can stimulate compassion and altruism
	Limits our link with the Divine	Necessitates our link with the Divine
	Keeps us from helping ourselves	Enables us to assist others and ourselves

	Sympathy	Empathy
Physical:	Can result in assumption of others' physical illnesses, aches, pains, and maladies	Promotes our ability to relate to others' physical problems
	Prevents us from diagnosing our own physical problems	Helps us diagnose others' physical conditions
	Robs us of our own immune functions; our antibodies are used for others' issues	Activates our immune responses to help self or other
	Sensitivity to objects can cause overwhelm and make it difficult to touch or wear anything	Awareness of energy in objects can help with discernment (when shopping, making, selling, sharing, or trading items)
Emotional:	Creates confusion between our emotions and those of others	Helps others clarify their emotions and emotional needs
	Causes us to repress our own emotions and needs (stuck emotions can lead to physical problems)	In helping others, we learn how to clear our own emotions and stress, thus improving our health
	Can eventually cause depression, anxiety, and lack of love	Increases our ability to bond
	Can limit success, as emotionally unavailable people are disliked	Enables friendship and success

	Sympathy	Empathy
Mental:	Creates mental disorders and anxiety	Can help others clarify their ideas, perceptions, interpretations, and needs
	Causes inability to discern our beliefs as separate from others	Creates clarity with personal beliefs
	Limits our success as we overpromote others' success	Enables mental bonding and use of our intelligence
	Mentally and intellectually supports others at cost to self	Mentally and intellectually supports others and self
Natural:	Easily overwhelmed by natural forces, animals' feelings, condition of plants and planets, and so forth	Feels at one with all things in nature
	Can't differentiate between own issues and those in nature	Can call on support of nature for health and wellness
	Negatively affected by planetary and cosmic events	Live attuned to planetary and cosmic events
	Natural forces intrude on life and health	Natural forces support life flow and ease

	Sympathy	Empathy
Spiritual:	Hard to trust people due to recognizing their hypocritical nature	Able to discern who to trust or not
	Exhausted from sensing difference between who someone is and should be	Supportive of others' paths, both current and potential
	Often perceived as judgmental	Able to accept all sides of a person
	Makes self responsible for others' ethics and morals	Able to give useful advice to others
Shamanic:	Can be overwhelmed by demonic forces	Can separate good from bad beings
	Can sense others' past lives; finds it difficult to separate current from past lives	Can provide insight to others regarding past lives
	Can feel constantly stressed by energy in a room	Able to perceive what has occurred and clear it
	Can end up possessed by dark forces	Can help others become free of dark forces

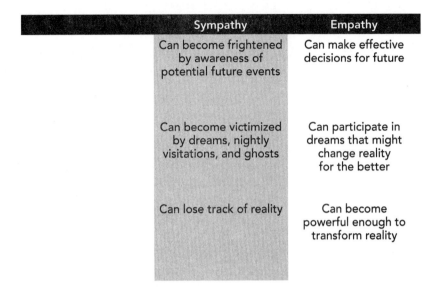

Sympathy	Empathy
Can become frightened by awareness of potential future events	Can make effective decisions for future
Can become victimized by dreams, nightly visitations, and ghosts	Can participate in dreams that might change reality for the better
Can lose track of reality	Can become powerful enough to transform reality

The Effects of Sympathy: Problems Abound

It has probably become evident that you don't want to sympathize rather than empathize. Yet if you've been more of a sympathizer than an empathizer up to this point in your life, don't feel bad. To hold on to energy rather than register it is often a practice we adopt when we are young children in reaction to our family environment. Plain and simple, we take in energy and hold on to it if doing so promotes our survival.

For example, we might take on a parent's physical maladies so they can better take care of us. We might load ourselves with a sibling's emotions so they cause our mother fewer problems. We might adopt Dad's beliefs so we can please him, or we might become environmentally sensitive in order to feel close to animals (the creatures of nature as a refuge). We might become hypersensitive to a parent's level of honesty so we know when they are lying to us, or we attune to spirits to mitigate a lonely childhood.

The resulting unconscious pattern of holding rather than registering energy is one that follows us into adulthood. It's not your fault if you had to survive through the sympathetic or enmeshment mechanism. The good news is that you can change your patterns by using the practices in chapter 5, restoring your ability to empathize in a way that is loving for others as well as yourself.

Sympathy can lead to more than the mere holding of energy. It is also the basis for some of the other experiences that masquerade as empathy, which you were introduced to in chapter 3. As you explore each of these experiences here, see if you remember ever confusing empathy with its false companions.

Personalization

Sometimes people believe they are empathizing with another when they are actually experiencing their own feelings. In a way, they are "borrowing" the other's feelings, senses, issues, or needs and playing off of them.

We can tell we are doing this when we find ourselves emoting or displaying more distress than the person we are supposedly relating to. For instance, we might be talking with a friend who lost her parent. She has tears in her eyes—and we are sobbing uncontrollably. Of course, it is natural to feel feelings or become emotional when we are empathizing. When personalizing, however, we become overly emotional.

In a way, we are stealing energy from the other person and asking them to suspend their own reality and needs in order to tend to us. We might even want them to take on our energy and thus feel sympathy for us, while unburdening us a little in the process. Personalizing another's experiences will cause them to feel hollow and unattended, and we will lose control.

Imagination

Many people struggle to differentiate imagination from empathy. When we empathize, we are truly sensing what someone or something else is going through. We don't make up the fact that someone else is physically ill or sad, in need of a pep talk or a hug. Yet we've all been guilty of letting our imaginations run wild to the point where we can convince ourselves of extremes, such as the idea that someone is really happy when they are sad or that an airplane our friend is on will crash the next day.

Sometimes our overactive imagination is a product of trying hard to stop a sympathetic tendency. To avoid being sympathetic, we unconsciously block all incoming information. It's like putting up a great big red stop sign to deflect all incoming data.

We can't function in the dark. Unless we are somehow able to relate to others or the external world, we end up feeling alienated and cut off. If we resist being sympathetic to the point of receiving zero to little data, our imagination might step in. It can create fantasies, possibilities, and even entire realms we perceive as real.

I've worked with many clients who are innately empathic but block this incoming information in order to avoid sympathetic tendencies. One was a man who insisted that his daughter was a stable, well-balanced, happy human being, no matter her obvious signs of trouble and instability. He only came to see me after the police had locked her into a mental asylum. Arrested for stealing, she had exhibited all the signs of manic depression and other serious mental disorders. Unconsciously, my client had refused to sense what was occurring with his daughter to such an extent that his lack of empathy was actually endangering her life.

Pity

Pity is literally defined as a sympathetic sorrow for one suffering or in distress. On the surface, it can feel beneficial to pity someone or ourselves, to give messages such as "poor you (me)" or "it's too much for you (me) to handle" or "no one could cope with what you are (I am) going through." Pity rather than empathy, however, can be seriously debilitating for whomever we are directing it to, including ourselves.

When we pity rather than empathize with someone, we energetically send the message that their troubles cannot be fixed. By expressing pity, we acknowledge that they are experiencing an overwhelming challenge or problem but also insinuate that the situation is hopeless. Worse, pity infers that there is nothing the Divine can do to help either, which leads to increased anxiety and depression and fosters irresponsibility. To affirm this stance will only increase the other person's misery, not point them toward responsible action or prayerful receptivity. Self-pity is equally injurious in that it tends to affirm the idea that there is nothing we can do to make our lives better; it's the great disempowerer.

Worse, pity opens us to take on another's problems. Believing that the other person cannot handle their life challenges or that the Divine cannot, we think we are sending compassion at first, only to invite their issues into our bodies in short order. Their pain is alleviated, but our own burdens are increased.

I often find pity at the core of abusive or addictive situations. I worked with a woman who greatly pitied her husband. He had a drug problem as a result of severe physical abuse during childhood. He also used his childhood problems as an excuse for being jobless while his wife worked, losing his temper with the kids, and gambling for money to feed his drug addiction. When I asked his wife why she tolerated his behavior, she said, "I feel sorry for him."

Likewise, we never do ourselves a favor by wallowing in self-pity rather than self-empathy.

Emotional Contagion

At first glance, emotional contagion might not sound like a big problem. It is a sympathetic process, however, that can lead to great woes.

Emotional contagion is usually defined as being swept up in another's feelings to the point that we go along for their ride, whether it's helpful for us or not. The most apparent example involves emotional sympathy, in which we pick up and coast on an individual's feelings. Perhaps our friend is sad, so we break down sobbing.

We can catch others' feelings and all other types of empathic information from individuals as well as groups. In the physical category, I once worked with a client who was ill with a kidney disease supposedly inherited from her family. Every member of her family had been diagnosed with this disease for two generations.

I suggested that she might have actually sympathetically absorbed this family disease rather than been born afflicted with it. Certainly she might be genetically predisposed, I affirmed, but what if there was more to it?

As soon as she decided to block the family kidney problem, her own kidneys healed.

Spiritual contagion can be especially dangerous. We have only to look to the rise of dogmatic and violent religious or political groups to see how far the affected can go. Hitler's regime, for instance, relied on his ability to snare his followers with the energy of Aryan spiritual principles. I believe the German people and other Nazi followers were subjected to waves and waves of hypnotic energy that they absorbed. The hook was the promise that these ideals would improve their lives. I also believe that any fanatic or fundamentalist religion or cult operates in the same way, dispersing spiritual dogma that is energetically absorbed by susceptible individuals.

Time and time again, I have worked with shamanically sensitive people who feel overtaken by otherworldly energies or beings. I once worked with a man who was a crack addict. He didn't want to do crack. He insisted, however, that every time he got money in his pocket, he could feel a dark energy enter his body and drive him to the streets in search of the drug. After doing crack, he would feel the dark force in his own body acting through him. As you can see from these examples, emotional contagion can have profound personal and collective consequences.

Hyperoptimism

Being optimistic is a good thing, isn't it? Don't scientific studies show that optimistic individuals tend to be happy and healthy rather than depressed and unhealthy?

Optimism is an uplifting quality, but this is not the case with hyperoptimism. We could define hyperoptimism as the insistence on predicting a beneficial outcome despite all odds, evidence, and indicators. At times we can actually lead others or ourselves into dangerous territory by being overly optimistic.

For instance, I once worked with a client who insisted that holistic therapies would guarantee a cure for her breast cancer. The cancer had started as a stage-one lump in her breast, which is highly treatable by allopathic surgery. No, my client said, all I have to do is change my diet and the malignancy will go away. Four years later, the cancer was stage four and had spread throughout her body, despite the fact that she had participated in one complementary practice after another. I believe my client's hyper-optimism prevented her from seeing the benefits of using both allopathic and complementary processes for a more integrative approach.

What was my client responding to? She was surrounded by people who believed in holistic treatments to the exclusion of allopathic medicine. Despite the fact that her family was worried about her, my client's system only took in the philosophy of this extremist group, filtering out any information that contradicted its overly optimistic promises.

We can take in energy that is physical, emotional, mental, natural, spiritual, or shamanic in such a way that we exclude the information that makes us feel pessimistic or negative. The problem with taking in only cheery data is that we're not getting the whole picture. We must also look at the dark side to make logical and effective decisions. Without looking at the potential costs or destructive outcomes, we can't effectively sift and weigh our choices to select the most realistic ones.

What Do Sympathy and the Other Empathy Impostors Look Like Energetically?

Want to picture what these states look like? Picture a ball of light.

This ball of light represents energy that is emanating from something or someone else and that you are being invited to respond to. You could decide to be empathic with this information: to register it and then respond with compassion. But maybe you're caught up in a sympathetic response and one of the following occurs:

SYMPATHY: The ball of energy passes completely into your body and rests in the area that is most susceptible to it. You now have the sense that this energy is entirely yours—physically, emotionally, mentally, naturally, spiritually, or shamanically. It then begins to play havoc with your life.

PERSONALIZING: The other person is expressing their emotional reality, and this triggers or calls forth your own issues or feelings. While they are expressing themselves, you create a ball of energy out of your own inner reality and basically duplicate what the other is going through. You might think you are responding to their process but, in fact, you are only feeling your own. At some point you might actually energetically hand your ball of energy to the other person, which is a way to ask them to care for you rather than you for them. In this way, you invite them to sympathetically carry your issues.

IMAGINATION: You can only take in bits and pieces of the ball of energy, and you build a false reality around these.

PITY: The ball of energy emanating from another enters your body and lands in the area where you are most vulnerable. You do not think the other person can handle it, so you take in the problem and try to fix it within your own body.

EMOTIONAL CONTAGION: The ball of energy enters you and lands in your area of sensitivity—and then passes right through, sweeping you up with it as it goes. You find yourself following the energy no matter where it leads you.

HYPEROPTIMISM: The ball of energy hovers in front of you. You take in only the positive messages, especially those that will lead to hopefulness, but not a full sense of another's reality.

In contrast, an empathic person will assure that the ball of energy stays outside their energy field and body. Instead, they accept the glimmer of energy that is projected off the ball. Remember our discussion about registering instead of absorbing another's energy? To register is to keep the ball's energy outside but let its light—the information it contains—shine in. If you start to feel overreactive, exhausted, too altered, or, conversely, totally shut down in response to someone else, the energy of the ball has penetrated or merged into your boundaries.

In the case of shutting down, you've most likely reacted to a potential invasion and subsequent loss of self by too tightly protecting yourself. Intuitively check to see where you are letting another's energy in, and use the techniques covered in this book to establish clear parameters. If you shut down too often, reflect on the reasons you might close off. By working on this fear pattern, you can decide to start registering information; after all, if you can keep the ball outside, you can be safely empathic. The shimmering energy of others' experiences can truly shine a clarifying light on the appropriate empathic understanding and response.

Sympathy and Radiant Empathy: When What We Take In Affects What We Send Out

Many of us respond to others' needs more energetically than we do concretely, actually serving as energy generators. When infected with others' energy, however, our radiant empathy ability is adversely affected; the held energy can block or warp the good energy we want to send.

For instance, imagine that you have taken in and are holding on to another's physical disease. The energy of this disease is stuck in your body, causing congestion. Now your system is not available to send healing to the other person. Worse, your own physical health runs down. You might actually exhibit the symptoms of the other person's disease and experience the exhaustion involved in trying to eradicate it.

The sympathetic bond, however, might create an energetic connection between you and the ill person. Picture this connection as a gigantic hose or tube—it is called a cord. The diseased energy continually pours into you. Your radiant empathy tendencies might now kick in and you find your healing energy automatically transferring to the other person, setting up a lose-lose cycle for you. You are continually taking on disease but sending healing energy to someone else.

A similar situation can occur with any of the empathic gifts if they operate sympathetically. Imagine absorbing another's depression to the extent that you can't feel anything but sad. One result is that you can't extend grace or care to anyone else who is sad because your own emotional radiant empathy is blocked. The other scenario involves the continual ingestion of another's sadness and the continual loss of joy—the antidote to sadness—as it passes from you to the person you are sympathizing with. As you can see, it's important at every level to stop sympathizing instead of empathizing, for your own well-being but also for the well-being of others.

We have all experienced sympathy instead of empathy. Personally, it took me decades of energetic and therapeutic work to figure out the difference, as I was raised in a family in which the other members benefited from my ability to absorb their emotions, illnesses, perceptions, and even spiritual issues and attachments. My safety and self-esteem were contingent on assisting my family members with their issues, essentially costing them the wisdom of working through their own issues—and me, the knowledge of my own needs. The most important step I took to use my empathic gifts in a useful way for others was to recognize my sympathetic tendencies. Self-awareness invites self-compassion and, eventually, self-healing.

APPENDIX 2

Impaired Empaths

*Are you then unable to recognize unless
it has the same sound as yours?*

ANDRÉ GIDE

Empathy is coded within us and threaded throughout us so that we might be touched by the world outside. We are designed for connection, created for love, and impassioned by compassion. As is true of everything applicable to the human condition, however, there are exceptions to the rule.

As we shall explore in this section, there are certain categories of people who are often described as being afflicted with "impaired empathy," a term used to signify empathic challenges. We are going to take a look at these broad groups, which include individuals labeled with mental, mood, and personality disorders, learning issues, and certain types of stress. We'll examine what research says about these challenges and the correlative role of empathy before drawing conclusions about how the empathic gifts might really work. We'll also examine beliefs about the causes of these disorders and the reasons why the empathic responses of those who have them might be impaired.

We'll also highlight the potential causes of impaired empathy, emphasizing reasons for it that you won't find in college textbooks. While this chapter will present the classical causes of impaired empathy, such as neurological and genetic challenges, to this list we will add reasons such as past-life issues and new scientific theories. We'll also examine how someone in a relationship with an impaired empathizer might be affected.

Impaired empathy usually presents as limited empathic gifts or even none at all, although sometimes being overempathic is also challenging. There are many reasons certain individuals or groups reveal impaired empathy. At one level, as we saw in chapter 2, our empathic gifts are biochemical in nature; if our bodies are unable to perform the functions involved in empathy, we will not be able to access our empathic gifts or will do so only partially.

Our empathic abilities are also electromagnetic. If our EMF faculties are skewed or problematic, our empathic abilities might also be skewed. Added to these physical-world reasons for empathic challenges are a host of others, including individual differences, family-of-origin upbringing, life experiences, training and education, soul issues, sympathetic overload, and more.

Before we jump in, I'm going to offer an important caveat. If you fit into any of the groups described in this chapter, know that there is hope. Being impaired (by normal standards) doesn't mean that you are a lesser person than others. Sometimes our lives appear adverse for a soul teaching. But sometimes the impairment really is too challenging for us. If this is the case, there are ways to shift our empathic reality through dedicated work or by accessing our empathy through different means. In part II of this book, we explored a variety of ways to enable healthier and more productive ways of being empathic.

Most importantly, I encourage you to read this discussion through the lens of love. Essentially, we are on this planet to learn about love. Some of us fall on one extreme of the continuum, suffering as supergifted empaths who would benefit from reducing our empathic exposure and involvement. Yet others dwell on the other side, with empathic abilities seemingly shut down and inaccessible. Wherever we fall on the spectrum, the ultimate goal is to listen to the music within our own souls as well as the souls of others, creating harmony as we move through this journey we call life—and enjoying the symphony together.

What Is an Impaired Empath?
(With a Caveat: No Shame Allowed)

The word *impaired* means "diminished in strength, quality, or utility." People who are impaired empathically have either a reduced ability to empathize or the opposite: an oversensitive emotional palate. Either side of the continuum can result in a diminished sense of self or a reduced ability to flourish and evolve.

Most of us can understand that being underempathic can present challenges. I once worked with a young boy named Kyle who was extraordinarily closed off. While he wasn't diagnosed as autistic, he had many of the same characteristics as people who are. He was almost nonresponsive to his family members' moods. He would hit his sisters in order to get a toy and be surprised by their tears. He seemingly had no sense of what was going on with others. His severe social challenges marked him as a critically impaired empath in danger of experiencing a lifetime of hard relationships.

But while Kyle was challenged when it came to emotional and mental empathy, he was a strong natural empath. Dogs, cats, guinea pigs—Kyle broke into a smile when they were happy and wiggly and frowned when they were sad or hungry. His inability to connect with people was costly to him and his loved ones. But his link with animal companions represented a way into his soul—and possibly into human relationships. Perhaps he and his loved ones couldn't share a toy or a ball, but how about a cuddle with a puppy?

Sometimes it's difficult to think of being overempathic, a condition also called being sensitive or oversensitive, as a problematic state—unless, of course, you are overempathic. As we've discussed many times, being too open in any of the six empathic areas can leave us feeling like a leaf blowing in a breeze—and not only lovely, light spring breezes; what about hurricanes? Feeling powerless to protect yourself against other people's dilemmas is a debilitating feeling indeed.

Clinical conditions and learning issues are mainly characterized as causing empathic impairment, and some people believe that the reverse is also true—that empathic problems might even cause some clinical conditions. People with diagnoses such as bipolar disorder and depression are typically described as being underempathic. But as you'll soon learn, this rigid assumption is being shaken. For instance, researchers are now considering that depression is at least partially caused by overempathic rather than underempathic tendencies.

At one level, most of us could be said to be empathically impaired. For example, you could say that an emotional empath who is unable to access the other five types of empathy is empathically impaired. Likewise, you could suggest that the shamanic empath, the person who struggles with boundaries on all levels, is impaired because the sheer scope of their empathic gifts causes them difficulties.

Because of the variance in empathic abilities and the different reasons that underlie empathic impairment, it is vital that we not attach shame to empathic conditions and challenges, whether or not the person with an empathic impairment can be labeled with a therapeutic or medical diagnosis. Certain conditions—especially biochemically based mental illnesses—are greatly affected by genetics and biological factors. Is this the fault of the person with the condition? Some situations, including anxiety and depression, might be rooted in physical factors but also be caused by upbringing, abuse, or situational stress. Still other issues, such as autism and ADHD, are clearly brain related.

At our core, we are all spiritual beings. Those of us who wear a clinical diagnosis on our lapel aren't "bad people," and individuals who don't wear one aren't "good people." In fact, mental illnesses are not rare. One in four adults experiences a mental health disorder every year, and one in seventeen lives with a serious mental illness.

Of the people who experience a lifetime mental illness, half begin facing it by age fourteen, and three-quarters by age twenty-four. Yet decades may pass between the onset of a mental health disease and receiving treatment.[47]

No matter our clinical state of mind and body, we are each an expression of the Divine, here to explain, expose, and enhance a particular form of love. And we are on earth to explore our divinity in very human ways, which include dealing with difficulties that may or may not place us in the "normal" category.

As we explore the different subgroups of impaired empaths, I encourage you to keep shame out of the picture. If love is the reason we are here, then love is the ultimate antidote for living with or transforming everything, including impaired empathy.

Classic Groups of Impaired Empaths

As empathy is classically defined as the ability to share and know the feelings or perceptions of another, several different groups of people are recognized as being empathically impaired.

Today's scientific research into impairment centers on the two main types of empathy. The first is emotional empathy, which researchers also term affective empathy. This is the type that inspires an appropriate emotional reaction to another. Then there is cognitive empathy, which is also called mentalizing, Theory of Mind, or social cognition in therapeutic terms. We will call this mental empathy because it invites mental perceptions.

Our exploration of impaired empaths will include several different types of mental disorders. We will also examine the broad categories of psychotic disorders and learning challenges and look at stress and post-traumatic stress disorder (PTSD).

Please understand that while these basic categories of impaired empaths are classically organized—that is, based on primary scientific and therapeutic knowledge—there are other ways of categorizing individuals and their symptoms, and there are gaping holes in our understanding of people with these issues. If you are interested in any of these topic areas or diagnoses, you will want to conduct further research or see a licensed professional. My goal with this appendix is for you to leave these profiles with a general sense of what might be occurring inside people who have empathic challenges.

Mental Disorders

There are several different types of mental disorders. These include anxiety, mood, personality, cognitive, psychotic, and substance-related disorders, as well as disorders of childhood and adolescence. Some professionals also have a separate classification for schizophrenia, delusional disorders, dissociative disorders, and sexual disorders. Many of these are characterized by empathy-related symptoms. We will be looking at a sampling of these disorders in relation to empathic impairment.

While throughout this book we worked with six different types of empathy, our discussion of mental disorders will be limited to the two types that are measured by researchers: anxiety and mood disorders.

Anxiety Disorders

Anxiety disorders are the most common of the psychiatric illnesses, affecting 15 to 20 percent of medical clinic patients. They are characterized by a sense of dread, unease, or foreboding.

There are hundreds of reasons we might feel anxiety. Anxious feelings could indicate a psychiatric condition or the reaction to a true threat such as a terminal illness or poverty.[48] A Stanford study has even linked anxiety to digestive irritation early in life.[49] When anxiety interferes with our daily life, it could be classified as a disorder.

While few studies probe the relationship between anxiety and empathy, many people believe that anxiety can be linked to overempathy. One group of researchers and therapists believes that many anxious people are actually highly sensitive people who comprise about 15 to 20 percent of our population. The highly sensitive person has a sensitive nervous system, causing them to pick up on what is occurring outside them. Because they absorb, reflect, and often dwell upon this incoming information, they are likely to become overwhelmed and, therefore, anxious.[50]

Many of the clients I work with report that they have been anxious since childhood. Some are emotionally or mentally empathic, but many are also able to pick up on entities and spirits, others' physical conditions, what is occurring in nature, and issues related to others' integrity and values. In short, I believe that many anxiety disorders are actually caused by hyperempathy.

For instance, one of my clients had taken nearly every antianxiety medicine available and nothing touched her nightly panic attacks. At first she refused to tell me why. I finally guessed that she was picking up on energy in her bedroom and surrounding spaces. After I questioned her, she admitted that she could feel the ghosts of her ancestors; in fact, several had been visiting her nightly since she was a child. My client's shamanic empathy was giving her anxiety. After we asked the Divine to heal and then remove these spirits, she reported that they were gone and her panic attacks had ended.

THE STRESS-INDUCED ANXIETY DISORDER:
New Thoughts on PTSD

We all go through bouts of stress that leave us exhausted and personally debilitated. This stress might be short term, acute, or chronic, but in any event, too much stress can sometimes close down our empathic abilities or, conversely, expand them to a hyperarousal level.

Prolonged stress is by far the most challenging in its effects on our mental health and our capacity for empathy. For instance, research shows that protracted stress in young children can slow or even stop brain development and physical growth as well as empathic functions.

One of the reasons for the disturbing effect of stress on our empathy is that our bodies respond to stress by releasing cortisol from the adrenals, which, if it happens over a prolonged period of time, causes long-term damage to the brain and immune system. In a child, repeated stress in the environment forms brain connections that cause them to react strongly to perceived threats. Even when the stressors are removed, the brain continues to act as if the threats are present, and the body basically becomes stuck sending SOS signals to the primitive parts of the brain. The brain stem in particular becomes overdeveloped, and areas responsible for emotional control and effective decision making are reduced. The result includes anxiety, poor impulse control, and a lack of empathy.[51]

The more frequently a child, or even an adult, is exposed to harmful or scary situations, the greater the chance that their empathy will become blocked. This is one of the factors behind post-traumatic stress disorder (PTSD), a severe anxiety disorder that can develop in children or adults after exposure to any event that results in psychological trauma. Severe PTSD can cause flashbacks and nightmares, challenges with falling or staying asleep, anger, and hypervigilance. Another common symptom is impairment in social functioning.[52]

There are numerous causes of PTSD. These include psychological trauma, involvement in war, being victimized by disaster, the diagnosis of a life-threatening illness in self or a loved one, being bullied or mobbed, and genetic predisposition. Our epigenetic material, if exposed to enough trauma, can toggle on the genes that suppress empathy or enhance it. The effects of PTSD might actually account for much of the trauma that underlies impaired empathy or related conditions.[53]

The research on PTSD only outlines the effects of debilitating stress on emotional and mental empathy, but our other four forms of empathy can be equally affected. I've met adults who could play Dr. Dolittle while growing up, walking and talking with the animals—or plants or ocean waves or the moon. With one client, the stress of ridicule shut down his intuitive abilities and made him an anxious and unhappy person. Once he reengaged his natural empathy, he discovered a peace of mind he'd never experienced before.

One of the empathic abilities frequently affected by PTSD is physical empathy. I find that trauma usually blows our instinctive physical empathy wide open or snaps it tightly shut. Clients with hyperphysical empathy are frequently sick, financially challenged, and have a hard time in primary relationships. They often attract underempathic individuals and feel guilty when they say no to abuse. They sponge so much energy from others that they can even feel the pain another person might experience if they were to suddenly stop absorbing all the other's problems.

On the other hand, victims of PTSD sometimes move their chairs to the other side of the continuum, deciding unconsciously that they would rather sense nothing in their bodies than reexperience the pain of an earlier time. These people exhibit symptoms that are more narcissistic or even psychopathic, sometimes using substances to keep numbing the scary pain. How can you be emotionally or mentally empathic with others if you can't even identify with your own body?

While PTSD can often be tracked to experiences in this lifetime, it can also be traced further back in time. I remember working with a client who was overly empathic in every area. She also presented all the symptoms of being a rape victim but, despite years of therapy, couldn't remember being sexually abused. We performed a past-life regression, and she recalled being gang raped in an earlier lifetime. As she processed through the horror of that experience, which was lodged in her soul, she was eventually able to manage her shamanic gifts so they didn't interfere with her life.

Every one of the reasons presented in the section titled "A Discussion of Causes of Empathic Impairment" later in this appendix can be a causal factor or carrier of PTSD. In addition to the areas we've already explored, what could be more traumatic than having a chunk of your soul locked away in someone else or attached to an entity? How much more severe is your own PTSD if it triggers an ancestral memory that was similar? How would your body respond to an interfering spirit that attaches to your primary cell, the first cell created at conception (and discussed later in this chapter)—the point being here that there can be many reasons for an empathy impairment challenge.

In the end, I believe that most impaired empathy has its roots in some form of PTSD, which makes it all the more important to track down the experience and heal it. You can do this by working with a professional and/or using the exercise "An Example of Healing: Freedom from PTSD" in chapter 6.

Mood Disorders

Mood disorders are disturbances in which an individual's moods become problematic. The two major categories are major depressive disorder and bipolar disorder. Each is linked to empathic impairment.

DEPRESSION (MAJOR DEPRESSIVE DISORDER)

We all feel sad or down once in a while, but a despairing mood that lasts more than a day or two may border on depression, the most common mental disorder in the world. In fact, the World Health Organization projects that by 2020 depression will be the major source of disability in the developed world and the second most important cause worldwide.[54]

Lingering sadness, when it interferes with daily life, is often called depression. The symptoms include a persistent sadness, anxiety, or sense of emptiness; feelings of hopelessness or worthlessness; irritability and fatigue; and sometimes thoughts of suicide or attempts on one's own life.

There are many different types of depression and just as many causes, including genetics, survivor guilt, chemical and hormonal imbalances, addictions, the illness of oneself or a loved one, loss, postpartum disorder, and seasonal affective disorder (SAD), caused by lack of sunlight.[55] In relation to empathy, however, many people believe that depressive individuals are not empathetic, probably because they often appear withdrawn or reclusive. However, researchers have now connected depression and empathy, pointing out that depressed individuals most frequently have normal, if not higher, levels of empathy relative to the mainstream population. Unfortunately, they also tend to unrealistically blame themselves for the pain other people feel. As is the case with most mood disorders, the depressed person's empathy system is functional; however, they are seemingly cursed with an overly active moral system set on automatic pilot.

This means that many depressed individuals experience an exaggerated reaction to others' difficulties and emotional problems. Rather than thinking about the present, they agonize over their perceived sins of the past or how they might be endangering the people they currently know. They are inherently prone to worry and guilt and tend to have developed a pathway for empathy early in life. But they struggle to think of helpful strategies for assisting others, so their connection between empathic concern and altruistic activities may be somewhat impaired or even severed.

These observations are leading many scientists to believe that mood disorders might often be caused by or result in an overly heightened sense of empathy.[56]

I often experience clients with depression as extremely empathic, and not only emotionally and mentally. One of my clients, who had been clinically depressed for years, was abused as a child, and prescription medicines and therapy hadn't touched her symptoms. She finally figured out that when she was growing up, she had overidentified with her parents, who were both physically abusive and alcoholics. She was literally filled with their feelings of self-loathing and sadness. Once my client decided that it wasn't her job to take on her parents' inner realities, her depression symptoms disappeared within days, although they often reappeared when she was around people who reminded her of her parents.

BIPOLAR DISORDER

An exciting scientific paper titled "Neuropsychological Evidence of Impaired Cognitive Empathy in Euthymic Bipolar Disorder" looks at a new way to examine bipolar disorder, namely via the lens of emotional and mental empathy.[57]

Bipolar disorder, also called manic depression, is characterized by mood swings that range between unbelievable highs and depressive lows. It is the fifth leading cause of disability worldwide, and the rate of suicide for people with bipolar disorder is sixty times higher than it is in the general public.[58] The word *euthymia* describes the middle or more "normal" range a bipolar visits when they aren't cycling high or low. This paper discusses the fact that even when they experience so-called normal emotions, people who are bipolar are still empathically impaired.

According to the authors of the paper, recent research indicates that an impaired theory of mind, or mental empathy, might not just be a sideline of bipolar disorder but could even cause the aberrant social behaviors that characterize the condition.[59]

How did the researchers figure this out? Mental or cognitive empathy and emotional empathy rely on two different areas of the brain. The researchers discovered that people with bipolar disorder were impaired in the cognitive brain areas but were highly functional in the emotional areas. This means that the bipolar individual has a hard time reflecting on the viewpoints of others but will feel anxious and tense in interpersonal settings because they have heightened awareness of emotions. This imbalance might account for their inability to regulate their emotional swings, partially because they cannot cognitively assess the real reasons that others are upset.[60]

I have found that people with bipolar disorder nearly always need medication to stop their mood swings, as well as therapy to deal with the deeper issues. I know a man who was eventually able to wean off his meds with the help of a professional therapist and a nutritionist, as well as a spiritual program, but I have not personally discovered a way to provide significant assistance through energy medicine.

However, from an intuitive point of view, I have often perceived a chasm in the soul or psyche of bipolar people. One person close to me rotated between extreme highs and lows. When he was at his low point, he was stuck in shame and unable to accept the fact that he was lovable.

When he was at his high point, he was unable to embrace his inner shadow or wounded child self, such was his grandiosity.

Many times I have perceived these splits between a person's "bad" and "good" parts as an early attempt to reunite the human and divine selves. I believe this chasm mirrors the disconnect between the emotional and mental aspects of empathy but also opens bipolar individuals to shamanic influences such as the invasion of or attachment to entities, or what is called interference. (See the section titled "Entities and Dark Forces" later in this appendix.)

I once watched a bipolar individual become possessed by an intruding entity. We were working on severe childhood wounds, including sexual molestation by his sister and abandonment by both his mother and father. His eyes, which were normally green, turned black as if a cloud was entering him, and he began to shout and swear at me, telling me that I was eroding his self-confidence and ruining his life. He had entered a manic state, characterized by fast talking, bragging, and grandiosity—and then he left my office. His wife later confirmed that this was how he responded anytime they became loving with each other.

Personality Disorders

There are a total of twelve personality disorders: paranoid, schizoid, schizotypal, antisocial, borderline, histrionic, narcissistic, avoidant, dependent, obsessive-compulsive, depressive, and passive-aggressive. Some include the psychopathic disorders in this grouping as well. We will emphasize psychopathic disorders, as various types of psychopathy are making the news more and more often: individuals on the extreme side of this continuum are often involved in brutal and painful situations and crimes. As we shall see, empathic issues are part of this critical disorder.

A person is usually diagnosed with one or many of these conditions when they frequently exhibit abnormal patterns of inner experience and behavior, and when they are frequently harmful to themselves or others. In other words, their thoughts and behaviors are not beneficial and have been pervasive for a very long time.

For our purposes, we're going to explore three of the better-known personality disorders—borderline, narcissistic, and psychopathy—and their relationship with empathy in order to further comprehend how the standard empathic gifts—in particular, the emotional and mental—might interplay with these challenges. We'll also look into different ways the other types of empathy can appear with these disorders.

Borderline

Individuals with borderline personality disorder (BPD) are unstable in personal relationships, self-image, and emotions. They are also usually quite impulsive and engage in frantic efforts to avoid being abandoned, even when the abandonment is imagined. Often consumed with anger, they are vulnerable to paranoia and excessive mood changes, which occur every few hours or days.

The causes of BPD are unknown, although most professionals believe that factors include biological and genetic, social (such as family of origin in source), and psychological, which includes a combination of personality traits shaped by learned (or not learned) coping skills.[61]

In relation to empathy, BPD is sometimes called "borderline empathy" because of a paradox in empathic behaviors. People with BPD can't always correctly interpret the verbal and nonverbal cues they receive from others; as a result, they believe others are trying to hurt them when they are not. But they can also sense another's current emotional state by astutely reading emotions, sometimes pinpointing a feeling that the subject isn't even aware of.

Research suggests that the borderline person is able to read the area around the eyes to determine another's mental state. This function is not present in conditions such as schizophrenia and autism.[62] Other research, however, reflects that borderlines are not empathic; in fact, they lack both emotional and mental empathy. Rather, it seems that they are so caught up in their own emotional experiences that they don't pay attention to what is occurring with others.

The research that might offer the most insight shows that impaired empathy might actually be the cause of BPD; neurological images support this claim. Instead of being empathic, people with BPD show emotional contagion or personal distress, meaning they are sharing emotions concerning themselves, not another. Both their mental and emotional empathic abilities are impaired.[63]

My understanding of borderline personality is that underneath the condition is extreme fear. What might a borderline be scared of? I have discovered that they are frightened about experiences in the past, but not the recent past. For instance, I worked with one borderline person who remembered his mother's terror of his father when he was in the womb. Yet another recalled a past life when he was a soldier in the Civil War and was killed, and another borderline remembered an ancestor's traumatic experience in war. At some level, I believe the borderline is still held prisoner in a terrifying episode from their own or another's experience base and doesn't know how to get out. You can't be empathic if you are only empathizing with your own wounded inner self, who distorts the perception of current situations to fit the past.

Narcissistic

Narcissistic personality disorder (NPD) is a mental condition in which people inflate their own importance because of an exaggerated need to be admired. Narcissists are characterized by an attitude of superiority, grandiosity, entitlement, and lack of empathy, although many narcissists are highly manipulative and can act like they are empathic.

It is not only individuals who are affected with narcissism. Several studies suggest that society overall is becoming increasingly narcissistic, with people encouraged to look out for themselves first and foremost. While self-seeking is a good thing, this is true only to a point. It also lessens a person's willingness to pursue common goals that benefit everyone, not just the self.

There are many potential causes for narcissism, which include parental rejection, childhood abandonment, or being excessively praised by parents, which, in turn, can lead to an overvaluation of the self. No matter the cause, the darkness marring narcissists, the hallmark of their affliction, is their lack of empathy for the pain they cause others.[64] Some studies show that narcissists don't empathize emotionally or mentally. Yet others reveal that they can access cognitive or mental empathy but are severely deficient in emotional empathy.[65]

And even while narcissists can fake empathy, one particular individual, an author who overcame narcissism, relays that he was able to transform his narcissistic diagnosis by learning how to truly listen to others. Ironically, one method he used was to turn others' words into his own inner voice, thus putting his narcissistic tendencies toward self-absorption to good use.[66]

I have personally worked with thousands of people who have been lost, hurt, and confused by their narcissistic family members, spouses, children, or friends—but also a few hundred individuals who would qualify as having narcissistic personality disorder. I have typically found that in the former case, the "non-NPDs," as they are called, are typically over-empathic and have a hard time breaking away from the narcissist because they can perceive the wounded child who exists within that person. They don't want to abandon the innocent child at the person's center, lying in wait beneath layers of sophisticated defenses.

Those narcissists who have shifted have allowed me to lift the lid off their protective mechanisms and seek out the wounded child within, the inner child huddled in a ball and hiding from others. Once they are able to share the deep pain within, they have opened like blossoming flowers to those around them.

Psychopathy

The word *psychopathy* comes from the ancient Greek word for *psyche*, which means "soul," and *pathos*, "suffering, disease, and condition." Many of us are scared of psychopaths, who are sometimes called sociopaths, because of their severe lack of empathy and the resulting harm they can cause.

Psychopathy presents as shallow and empty emotions (especially reduced fear), the ability to tolerate stress beyond a normal capacity, coldheartedness, selfishness, lack of remorse or guilt, superficial charm, a manipulative personality, irresponsibility, and, above all, a lack of empathy. Psychopathic behaviors, however, exhibit on a continuum. On one side are the high-functioning psychopaths who often end up high on the corporate ladder or holding a political seat. Their lack of care for others doesn't stop them from climbing their way to the top.[67] On the other side are the psychopaths that are the subject of so many Hollywood movies, often called sociopaths: those who are so antisocial that they end up in a parasitic or criminal lifestyle.

Research has now shown that psychopaths have a deficit in their ability to empathize, which leads to a lack of moral judgment.[68] They actually enjoy causing fear in others because the fear centers in their brains are dysfunctional, causing the more extreme sociopaths to chuckle when others are scared. The reduced activity in these regions of the brain during fear-provoking situations leads to lax moral behavior.[69]

While bullying hasn't been clearly defined as a psychopathic behavior, research shows that bullies also enjoy seeing others in pain. Brain scans show a disruption in the natural empathic response of bullies, which suggests that the rationale behind their cruelty is similar: scaring others provides these individuals with a sense of power.[70]

And yet, researchers from the Netherlands have recently determined that psychopaths can actually turn empathy on and off, as measured by brain chemistry. They seemed to be able to become empathic when they were told to study others being empathic. This research suggests that psychopaths don't lack empathy; rather, their empathy is abnormally suppressed.[71]

What exactly causes psychopathy? The theories include biological nature, genes affected by abusive environments, social forces, natural selection, and brain damage. I believe we must add past-life influences to this list, as I have worked with psychopaths who have been shut down from birth. In addition, I believe that some psychopathic situations are caused by soul fragmentation, the subject of a section appearing later in this chapter. I once worked with a psychopath who had kept his "feeling self" outside his body his entire life because a particular past life had been so traumatic. Once he integrated this part of his soul, he became softer and more caring. However, he also had to work with a therapist to learn how to identify his emotions, as genuine feeling was new to him.

Substance-Related Disorders

Substance-related disorders are extremely common, unfortunately, and we would require a tome to even begin a decent discussion of them. For our purposes, however, we will consider the two main categories of substance-related issues:

- substance abuse, which involves dependence on harmful substances, including alcohol, drugs, nicotine, inhalants, prescription medicines, and more
- substance-induced disorders, which encompass intoxication, withdrawal, and psychiatric syndromes that develop as a result of using a substance

In general, people are considered substance abusers if they continually use a substance despite significant problems caused by its use. Substance abuse and substance-induced disorders can both lead to the development of psychosis, anxiety, and other issues. As well, individuals can use substances to assuage mental illness, childhood abuse, and more.

One of the more serious side effects of addiction (not only to substances but to work, sex, rage, food, and more) is the effect on those in relationship with the addict. One of the chief complaints of loved ones is that the addict shows no empathy; in fact, they don't seem to even care about their loved ones. The addict is often so self-consumed that they have lost all compassion for others' needs and the effects their negative behavior has on others.

Research shows that although the addict might care deep inside, their empathy is held hostage by the addiction. They are also frequently unable to recognize or describe their own feelings; in fact, nearly 40 percent of all alcoholics have alexithymia, a psychological syndrome in which the person cannot identify their own feelings. Even after drug rehabilitation, an alcoholic is less empathic than other people, especially in the acute period right after detoxification.

The burning question is whether impaired empathy came before the substance abuse or after—or if both occurred at once. Research shows that callous and unemotional children are at greater risk for antisocial behavior (psychopathic tendencies) and substance abuse. But others say that the lack of empathy can also follow the use of the substances. It does seem that one of the reasons that twelve-step programs like Alcoholics Anonymous and Al-Anon can be helpful is that empathic skills are relearned through the group experience.[72]

I have considerable experience in dealing with addicts through my own practice. I have usually found that alcoholics were often highly empathic as children but family circumstances or trauma sidelined the continued development of their empathy. I have worked with several clients who actually used drugs to block their empathic abilities, including all six forms of empathy.

I also believe that substances each run on their own vibrational frequencies and can attract dark energies or entities that continually entice the addict to use the substance. An example is the client I described in appendix 1 who was a crack addict: a voice, not his own, insisted that he get high and plagued him until he used.

I think this sort of shamanic empathy might be latent in many substance abusers, those who unconsciously form a sort of alliance with a negative energy in order to hide from their own inner pain. My opinion is that parents should be taught the various types of empathy and the sensitivities associated with them so they can help their children be protected yet open to their gifts.

Psychotic Disorders

Psychotic disorders are a group of serious illnesses that affect the mind, altering the ability to make effective decisions, think and communicate clearly, behave appropriately, or be emotionally empathic. The best known include the various schizophrenic disorders, which are described here.

Schizophrenic Disorders

Schizophrenic disorders are characterized by difficulty in distinguishing between what is real and unreal, managing emotions, relating to others, and thinking clearly. Some forms of schizophrenia involve hallucinations and similar illusory experiences. Overall, schizophrenia is considered a brain disorder that causes so much blurring between the perception of reality and actual reality that people with the condition often withdraw from the world. Impaired empathy is a component of the condition.

Studies, including one entitled "Schizophrenia Patients Are Impaired in Empathic Accuracy," show that compared with controls, schizophrenic people show lower empathic accuracy than others. They are often unable to accurately figure out what others are feeling based on their emotional expressions or social cues.[73] The seeming lack of empathy doesn't mean that the schizophrenic cannot be empathic. *The Harvard Medical School Family Medical Guide* states that people with this condition reveal a full range of emotions, but the paranoia and distrust associated with the condition might cause them to withdraw.[74]

Some of the less traditional approaches to schizophrenia include seeing it as an acute psychospiritual crisis. Dr. Maureen Roberts, whose doctoral thesis embraces C. G. Jung's theories, suggests that the condition is caused by personality fragmentation, a loss of the sense of self, and *extreme* empathy and environmental sensitivity, rather than the opposite, or reduced empathy. She believes it is a soul issue, one that needs to be approached as holistically as possible.[75]

Revealing the strong association between our physical and psychological selves, yet other research is linking the development of schizophrenia to prenatal infections with influenza, the need for additional vitamins and minerals such as vitamins C and B3, and genetics.[76] Environmental factors can also play a role, as can stress, drug abuse, and major life changes. There also seems to be a production of too much dopamine, a neurotransmitter, which can lead to delusions.[77]

From the point of view of the empathic lens, schizophrenic empathy is indeed a complicated matter. I have frequently worked with schizophrenics and often find that a contributing factor includes shamanic empathy, with a slight twist. The schizophrenics I've met or worked with have heard voices, been plagued with intrusive visions, or had the sense of other presences. I believe that early childhood violations or extreme challenges, or sometimes carried-in traumas from past lives, have caused the souls of some of these clients to be halfway out of their bodies.

Imagine that your soul looks like a human being. Your soul's feet should be all the way in your physical feet. Energetically, in relation to the schizophrenics I've worked with, the soles of their souls are at chest level, if not higher, leaving the better part of their souls up and out of the body. Lacking the boundary of physicality, the upper part of the soul is vulnerable to shamanic influences such as entities, and the bottom half to the sympathetic absorption of others' energies.

I have the sense as well that some of the entities or energies that plague certain schizophrenic individuals might be parts of their own souls. The traditional shaman is a soul healer, often performing healing by finding and reintegrating the fragmented or lost parts of the soul, which might become splintered off from the larger soul because of trauma, tragedy, or even misunderstandings.

The second type of empathy that might affect the schizophrenic condition is spiritual. I have often found that people with schizophrenic tendencies are highly sensitive to others' spiritual issues. For instance, one of my schizophrenic clients can always tell when someone is lying or being hypocritical. She spends a vast amount of time trying to figure out who is hypocritical and who isn't. I believe that this sensitivity can be found in many people who are anxious, schizophrenic, or otherwise deemed psychologically unhealthy, and to such an extent that it presents challenges.

The third type of empathic connection that can interfere with a schizophrenic's life is physical. Because another's energy can occupy the empty places in the schizophrenic's body, they can be potentially vulnerable to exhibiting others' illnesses and problems.

Learning Challenges

Of ever-growing concern are two conditions that hit the media—and our lives—with increasing frequency in regard to empathy. These areas are autism spectrum disorders (ASDs) and attention deficit hyperactivity disorder (ADHD), which we will more fully discuss in this section.

WHEN MIRROR NEURONS AREN'T ENOUGH:
A Reflection on Autism

One of the more heart-wrenching and confusing conditions facing humanity is autism, a disorder that describes a certain set of nonsocial behaviors. Autism is officially given the name autism spectrum disorder, or ASD. ASD is a general term for a group of complex brain disorders that present as difficulties in social interaction and verbal and nonverbal communication challenges. As well, many ASD children have problems with repetitive behaviors such as head banging, intellectual disabilities, motor skill challenges, and sleep and gastrointestinal disturbances, although they often excel in visual skills, music, math, and art.[78]

One of the most common descriptions of children with autism, as well as those with one of its better-known subcategories, Asperger's syndrome, is a lack of empathy. Studies actually show that 85 percent of ASD individuals have alexithymia, which involves not just the inability to verbally express emotions but also the inability to identify emotional states in self or others.[79] But some researchers, such as autism expert Phoebe Caldwell, suggest that individuals with ASD don't lack empathy; rather, they are too emotionally sensitive and suppress their emotional facility in order to avoid pain. Thus, the difficulty lies in expressing empathy rather than registering it.[80] This tracks with my own experience with ASD, that individuals with this challenge are hyperempathic rather than less empathic. While this issue is critical to resolve, the end result is the same. ASD individuals often have few to no social skills. One of the most crippling effects of this is that they have great difficulty making friends or inviting understanding from others.

There are various theories about the cause of autism and the apparent lack of empathy toward self or other, or at least the access to empathic or compassionate expression. Many studies reveal a problem in the interaction between their mirror neurons (discussed in chapter 4) and their brain waves. ASD individuals have mirror neurons, but they are effectively cancelled out by a mishap in the brain. This brain wave pattern, called a mu wave, has a frequency range of 8 to 13 hertz. When the mirror activity is high in the premotor centers of the brain, our mu rhythms are repressed—unless we have ASD. In autistic individuals, the mu rhythms are enhanced rather than suppressed when the individuals are performing tasks that typically toggle on the mirror neurons and empathy, thereby inhibiting mirror neuron functioning.[81]

THE ACTIVE AND ALERT EMPATHS:
About ADHD

Individuals with attention deficit hyperactivity disorder often have poor impulse control and short attention spans. The condition is often linked with other learning issues such as dyslexia and auditory processing difficulties, which cause major learning challenges for the ADHD person. ADHD people, especially those high in the hyperactivity factor, are often seen as low in empathy because they can come across as aloof, self-centered, or so lacking in impulse control that they are offensive to others.

The causes attributed to ADHD include genetics, neurological anomalies, brain chemical imbalance, viral infections, toxins, the mercury in vaccines, food additives, lead poisoning, faulty child raising, and more. Yet other studies are showing that in the case of ADHD, there might be inadequate bonding with the mother, resulting in a disorganized pattern of attachment. Other causes include exposure to trauma, which could involve abuse experienced by the mother when she was pregnant. The subsequent stress in the pregnant mother creates neurological pathways resulting in hypersensitivity and hyperarousal.[82] For this reason, certain researchers substitute the word *attachment* for *attention* in the name of the disorder.

One outcome for a child whose ADHD might have originated from a challenging family environment is that lacking consistent care from caregivers, he or she might be capable of hurting others without remorse.[83] Yet another is that some ADHD people might simply lack social skills.

My experience with ADHD individuals is that they are actually quite empathic, to the point of being very alert and active, but they can lack the ability to regulate their emotions. In fact, I believe that in the case of being raised by an abused and abusive mother, they might awaken their empathy early in order to protect the mother, thus shutting down other parts of their brains. As a case in point, there is currently a trend to change the ADHD title to focus on the auditory processing deficiency aspect, which means that the left brain is challenged to keep up with the right brain. Thus the ADHD person is actually constantly streaming empathic data, especially emotional and intuitive information, but is unable to identify and categorize it quickly enough.

My own son is highly ADHD and dyslexic, and I find him to be one of the most empathic individuals on the planet. When he was four, one of his caregivers said of him, "I am happy to have met one of the world's greatest humanitarians." His struggles involve figuring out how to capture everything he senses, feels, and notices, all of which call on his innate natural empathy.

Often, both ASD and ADHD people are highly responsive to animals and other companions. I have perceived an affinity that goes both ways, a bond of trust that easily develops between the learning challenged and the animals, especially intelligent and loving animals such as dogs, horses, and dolphins. We must wonder whether ASD and ADHD are always deficiencies rather than extensions of certain empathic abilities that need to be recognized and cultivated.

A Discussion of Causes of Empathic Impairment

We have already introduced a few of the potential causes for empathic impairment in this chapter. The most standard and classical factors have been these: neurological dysfunctions, brain chemistry anomalies, genetics, microbial infections, attachment disorders, faulty upbringing, inherent personality issues, lack of modeling, digestive issues, additives or other toxic poisoning, and trauma. But I have also mentioned past-life influences, soul wounds or fragmentation, interacting with entities or dark forces, oversympathy, and even experiencing ancestors' memories.

In this section I want to further explore the less traditional reasons that might underlie empathic impairment, including the nontraditional explanations I just listed. To this I add a handful of other potential causes, including two new areas of scientific study called epigenetics and primary cell theory. We will also expand on our conversation about oversympathy.

Past-Life Influences

Millions of people worldwide believe in reincarnation, the theory that we have been incarnated before this lifetime. While the religions of the Western world tend to scoff at the idea, profound spiritual and religious disciplines including Hinduism, Buddhism, Sikhism, Jainism, and many indigenous populations embrace the idea. There is even evidence in the New Testament that the Hebrew people contemporary to Jesus might have believed in reincarnation.

During an event often labeled by Christians as the Transfiguration, Moses and Elijah, who were long dead, appeared before Jesus and several others on a mountain, as described in the seventeenth chapter of Matthew. The Jewish people had also wondered if Jesus was the return of Moses or Elijah. In reading the Jewish historian Flavius Josephus, we also hear the echo of a belief in reincarnation, with Josephus stating that the souls of good men will return to other bodies, at which point they will have "the power to revive and live again."[84]

In relation to emotional impairment, the belief in reincarnation opens another source for the wounds and traumas that can affect our current condition, including those causing impaired empathy. For instance, I once worked with a young man with Asperger's syndrome. The story I intuitively received was that he was scared to empathize with others because he had witnessed the death of his entire family in a past life. By refusing to connect with loved ones in this life, his soul reasoned that it might be spared equivalent feelings of loss.

In the same vein, I once worked with a man with severe ADHD who had been a medicine man in a past life. Many of the villagers under his charge had died from smallpox. He had felt extraordinarily guilty for not having been able to predict the infection or prevent their deaths and had pledged that he would be hyperaware of others' needs and issues during his next life so as to prevent a further disaster. And was he ever hyperaware—of everything and everyone! His ADHD calmed down once he released this goal, and he was able to relax into his current life.

I believe past-life traumas are often carried on our souls, which then program our minds, our bodies, and our genes for certain ways of interaction. Thus, I believe our souls can actually influence which genes are turned on and off in our bodies, thereby creating the neurological and chemical conditions for impaired empathy. In a similar way, a successful past life, as it pertains to empathy, can encourage a certain type of empathy.

Soul Fragmentation

Soul fragmentation relates to the theory that illnesses, including emotional and mental ones, can be caused by a split or fragmentation of the soul, the part of us that incarnates lifetime after lifetime to learn about love.

There are many expressions of a fragmented soul. A soul can entirely vacate the body or never completely enter at conception or birth, leaving the person open for possession by negative energies or even occupation by another soul or entity. A soul can also split into two or more parts.

There are several places we can find a soul fragment. A soul part might be stuck in a past life, reexperiencing the loop of a past-life trauma over and over. It can be lost inside another person, held captive by an entity, or hidden inside of a part of our body. As suggested, it might even be dangling outside our body, not too certain that it wants to enter. As related to empathic impairment, soul fragmentation can explain why people are unable to experience empathy or are overly empathic.

For instance, a sociopath might be unable to relate to another person's needs because a part of their soul is outside rather than inside their body. The externalized part of the soul might contain the sociopath's emotions and feelings. How can you feel for another what you are unable to feel inside yourself? A depressed person might be holding a piece of someone else's soul, weighed down by that person's sadness or anger, feeling guilty because they are unable to make a real difference for them.

We might be plagued by an anxiety disorder because we are missing a vital part of our soul, perhaps an aspect that understands how to protect itself from others, or we may be haunted by schizophrenia because a part of someone else's soul keeps entering our body and exposing us to its chaotic imaging. No matter what might have happened to this part of us that bridges our humanness to spirit, healing a splintered soul is very similar to healing any other wounded part of ourselves. Having gone through or observed trauma, our soul splits and needs to be gently put back together again, with love being the thread that binds all wounds.

Entities and Dark Forces

There are many terms for the intrusion and effects of "dark forces," or invisible beings and energies that can plague us. Common phrases describing various phenomena that can cause harm to or stop our spiritual progression and maturation include spiritual interference, entity hauntings, ghosts, phantoms, ancestral hauntings, spiritual intrusion, or the influence of the dark (*dark* being a word used generically to name all invisible energies that seek to control us).

Soul fragments are often attached to negative entities, which seek to keep us split so as to better control us. Dark forces can also encourage the use of addictive substances or behaviors to keep us enthralled or disempowered. I believe that dark forces also encourage narcissism, as a person unable to care for others cannot fulfill their spiritual mission. (Our personal calling always includes being of service to others.) If we cannot care for others, a process that requires empathy, the dark forces, rather than the emissaries of the light, are better served.

Sometimes the dark entities encourage overempathy, tipping us into the sympathy zone. If we're burdened with others' pains or ills, it's hard to focus on our own needs and, therefore, our own purpose. It's hard to fulfill our destiny if we are overwhelmed with energies that are not our own.

In short, almost any empathic impairment can involve the intrusion of dark forces whose ultimate objective is to steal our energy. Why would they do this? Perhaps they are scared of the Divine, the ultimate source of light. They believe that they will be rejected, judged, or thrown into hell. Maybe an entity is itself wounded and afraid of the healing process. Or maybe an entity seeks revenge because that is an easier path through its pain than to be remorseful. For whatever reason, dark intruders can encourage both under- and overempathy in order to seek personal gain.

The Energy of Others:
The Dark Side of Sympathy

As appendix 1 illustrates, we can often be too sympathetic. When our empathic abilities are hyperaroused, we respond quickly to other energies. We can also go a step further and actually take these energies into our body.

I believe one of the most serious questions to ask when dealing with the conditions underlying impaired empathy is this: *are we responding to our own energy or someone else's?* While we must take personal responsibility for our own lives and behavior, it is also important to ask ourselves if the basis of our challenges started within or outside ourselves.

For instance, I worked with a man whom a therapist had diagnosed with narcissistic personality disorder. It's quite uncommon for narcissists to actually be diagnosed, as they often blame their problems on others in their need to perceive themselves as perfect (often storming out of therapy offices with great panache). However, this man wanted to change.

We discovered that his inner child was in a fetal position deep inside of him, originally injured by parents who fought day and night and literally called him worthless. A further force was imprisoning him as well: his dad's rage.

The rage my client's father exhibited during parental screaming matches had taken root inside him. Every time the inner child poked his head out to attempt to connect with others, the dad's energy would start to yell— and so, too, would my client at the person offering love. My client made true progress with his therapist after we removed his father's energy.

Epigenetics: The New Gene Theory

Scientists used to believe that genes held the secrets to our behaviors and illnesses. In actuality, though, only about 2 percent of our genetic material is actively working. The other 98 percent is called "junk DNA"— but it isn't junk. It serves a vital function.

This junk DNA, which mainly consists of viral and other microbial material, is one factor in a chemical soup that switches our genes on and off. The material with this toggling ability is called our epigenetic inheritance or epigene matter.

Depending on what we are exposed to in our environment, the factors in our epigenes can emit various reactions that can suppress or activate certain genes. Some of these epigenes contain the codes of our junk DNA's microbial history, but they are also infused with our ancestors' memories. When triggered, viruses, other microbes, or our ancestral memories, feelings, and experiences can cause a chemical reaction in our bodies, which in turn causes our genes to change. Scientists are starting to believe that this epigenetic activity might be behind many challenging issues, including cancer, immune disorders, and even neuropsychiatric disorders such as autism. In fact, nearly all conditions related to empathy can also be based in epigenetic issues, which can suppress or activate the genes controlling our empathic reactions.[85]

Primary Cell Theory

Dr. Grant McFetridge has developed a revolutionary theory and related therapeutic practice that have made major inroads into healing mental illnesses as serious as schizophrenia. He postulates that at a certain stage of embryonic development, we develop a primary cell that embodies our full consciousness. The seven major organelles, or cellular structures, developed by this stage are, in fact, each linked to a major aspect of self, including our chakras, meridians, and mind.

According to McFetridge, the stage immediately before this primordial cell development is one in which individuals develop the potential for schizophrenia, which is caused by an incomplete integration of the first seven basic cellular structures. In this gap we can be influenced by entity interference, the memories of our ancestors, or even our own past-life issues. Other life issues, including medical challenges (such as those that are linked with impaired empathy), can occur because of epigenetic damage in the primary cell and other cellular damage. Because this cell remains throughout our life, we can still work on it through energetic work and intention.[86]

Being in Relationship with an Impaired Empath: What's It Like?

Many of us have been or currently are in relationships with impaired empaths. While the configurations are endless, one of the most common scenarios is women in relationship with underempathic men.

At the extreme level, these men often display the symptoms of depression, substance abuse, personality disorders, severe ADHD, or even psychopathy. Their female mates are often the opposite: highly empathic and caring. (While the situation can be reversed—an empathic man partnered with an under- or impaired empathic woman, I'm painting the picture from its most typical view.)

Complaints from these women include having partners who constantly berate or ignore them, slight or belittle them, and don't care about their feelings, especially those they personally hurt. Outsiders constantly wonder why women remain with these men.

One of the reasons is actually genetic. From a neurological point of view, women don't seem to assess threats well. Instead, the chemicals in their bodies tell them to be *more* (rather than less) social. This means that a man can be dangerous or cruel and a woman will increase her interactions with him. In general, research shows that women share their own empathic impairment: they are hyperempathic, wired to care about others.[87] In my own practice I continually find that women are highly sensitive to the inner wounds in others and often suffer because of it.

For instance, one of my clients, married to a clear sociopath, wouldn't leave him because she knew he wasn't whole—a part of him simply wasn't there. She couldn't imagine abandoning him the way everyone else had. Yet another of my clients was subjected to continual neglect from a narcissistic boyfriend who also had borderline tendencies. He would break up with her every two weeks or so and then return, spying on her emails to make sure she hadn't taken up with anyone while he'd been footloose and fancy free. She didn't want to break up because she could see his wounded inner child, the one abandoned by a narcissistic mother.

I have also worked with men who remain attached to underemotional women. One client stuck with his narcissistic wife despite the fact that she cheated on him half a dozen times. While he said that he didn't want to disturb their children, the truth was that he was scared of how she would react if he left her. A spiritual empath, he was well aware of her hypocritical nature. Despite the fact that she was religious, he sensed that she would rake him over the coals if he filed for divorce. His predictive sense proved accurate; she battled him in court for two years after he finally left, accusing him of adultery even though she was the guilty party.

Certain overempaths eventually develop their own special syndrome called "caregiver burnout" or "caregiver fatigue." After professionally or personally caring for ill individuals, including people who are mentally ill, caregivers often close down and withdraw into a cocoon of exhaustion. In fact, one study shows that caregivers of the depressed often begin to mirror those they are helping, assuming the position of being overly responsible and guilty for the other's depression. They withdraw and sometimes blame the depressives for their troubles. Depression can therefore be seen as contagious, affecting all it touches, even loved ones and mental health caregivers. Overall, individuals who are sensitive to stress or problems in others are more prone to illness, distress, and hardships.[88]

The other side of the coin relates to individuals in relationship with overempaths or sympathizers, those who often feel controlled, confused, or overwhelmed by their loved one's sensitivities. To the underempath, or even the so-called normal empath, relating to a strong empath can be challenging.

I once worked with a man who was thinking of divorcing his wife. He swore that they were awake every night till two because she could hear the ghosts in the room. A disbeliever, he didn't understand what she was talking about. In fact, he pretty much thought she was crazy.

I treated someone else who didn't know how to handle her daughter, who could talk with animals. This mother was concerned that when her daughter went to school, she would be made fun of if she talked about what the mice in the walls were whispering.

We have just explored the oft-painful landscape of impaired empathy. The truth is that at some point in our lives, we will probably all struggle personally with at least one of the issues involving impaired empathy. And we will find our hearts stretched to capacity by others with concerns reflecting impaired empathy. We needn't be scarred by these experiences; rather, they are opportunities to embrace our humanity, the very reason empathy is so important. To feel is to heal.

Glossary

ALTRUISM—choosing to alleviate the suffering of another simply because it's the right thing to do; compassion in action

ANXIETY—a sense of dread, unease, or foreboding

ASPERGER'S SYNDROME—a subcategory of autism

ATTENTION DEFICIT HYPERACTIVITY DISORDER (ADHD)—a condition characterized by poor impulse control and short attention spans

AURIC FIELD—an energy structure surrounding the body that facilitates receiving and sending energy

AURIC LAYERS—layers of the auric field; each layer protects us and filters different types of information while transmitting particular data to the world around us

AUTISM SPECTRUM DISORDER (ASD)—a complex brain disorder that presents as difficulties in social interaction and verbal and nonverbal communication challenges

BIPOLAR DISORDER (ALSO CALLED MANIC DEPRESSION)—mood swings that range between unbelievable highs and depressive lows

CHAKRAS—a set of energetic bodies, seven of which are based in the physical body, each linked with a specific endocrine gland and section of the spine, with an additional five outside the physical body; unrestricted by space or time, they transfer physical or sensory energy into spiritual energy, and vice versa

CLAIRAUDIENCE—the spiritual gift of clear hearing

CLAIRCOGNIZANCE—the spiritual gift of clear knowing

CLAIREMPATHY—the spiritual gift of clear feeling (also called clairsentience)

CLAIRGUSTANCE—the spiritual gift of clear tasting

CLAIRS—a shorthand term for all the spiritual gifts

CLAIRSCENT—the spiritual gift of clear smelling

CLAIRSENTIENCE—the spiritual gift of clear sensing

CLAIRTANGENCY—the spiritual gift of clear touching

CLAIRVOYANCE—the spiritual gift of clear seeing

COMPASSION—the inner call to ease another's pain

COMPATHY—the shared ("com-") feelings ("pathy") of physical empathy

DEPRESSION—persistent, debilitating sadness, emptiness, or hopelessness

ELECTROMAGNETIC FIELD (EMF)—the electrical and magnetic energies emanating from the atoms, molecules, cells, and organs that make up your physical self

EMOTIONAL CONTAGION—getting caught up in the emotional energy of a group; one of the empathy impostors

EMOTIONAL EMPATHY—feeling another's feelings as if they were your own

EMOTIONAL INTELLIGENCE—the ability to reason about emotions and use feelings to enhance higher thinking

EMPATHIC GIFTS—the psychic, energetic abilities that facilitate the subtle-body experience of empathy

EMPATHIC STYLE—one of six modes of experiencing empathy that utilize the spiritual gifts; the modes are physical, emotional, mental, natural, spiritual, and shamanic

EMPATHY—the capacity to share and understand others' emotions and needs as if they were our own

EMPATHY DEFICIT DISORDER (EDD)—the inability to step outside ourselves and tune in to others' experiences, especially those who differ from us in feeling and belief

ENDOCRINE GLANDS—secreting organs distributed throughout the body; part of the bodily matrix (including mirror neurons and the brain) that invites empathy and compassion

FIVE STEPS TO COMPASSIONATE EMPATHY—one of the three tools for safely developing empathic gifts (see chapter 5)

HEALING STREAMS OF GRACE—beams or strands of unconditional divine love; one of the three tools for safely developing empathic gifts (see chapter 5)

HYPEROPTIMISM—acting happy to make a sad person feel better; one of the empathy impostors

IMAGINATION—conceptualized empathy, including make-believe empathic behaviors such as crying with someone or sighing at their pain; one of the empathy imposters

IMPAIRED EMPATHY—difficulty with empathy, which can manifest along a continuum from being too empathic to being closed off to empathy

MENTAL EMPATHY—receiving information and data from the outside world and seeming to simply "know" what someone else knows

MENTAL MALADJUSTMENT—using the empathic process in a maladjusted or manipulative way in order to meet one's own needs; one of the empathy impostors

MERIDIANS—rivers or channels of energy that flow through the body delivering subtle energy to all parts of it (similar to nadis)

MIRROR NEURONS (EMPATHY NEURONS)—nerves that allow us to mirror others' activities and reflect sensations and feelings; part of the bodily matrix (including the brain and the endocrine system) that invites empathy and compassion

MOOD DISORDER—a disturbance in which an individual's moods become problematic; two major categories are depression and bipolar disorder

NADIS—rivers or channels of energy that flow through the body delivering subtle energy to all parts of it (similar to meridians)

NARCISSISM—a mental condition in which people inflate their own importance because of an exaggerated need to be admired

NATURAL EMPATHY—relating to nature-based forces and creatures

PERSONALITY DISORDERS—mental conditions involving abnormal patterns of inner experience and behavior harmful to oneself or others; examples are paranoia, schizophrenia, and obsessive-compulsive disorder

PERSONALIZING—not experiencing the other's issues at all, but instead feeling our own feelings, needs, issues, and reactions; one of the empathy impostors

PHYSICAL EMPATHY—the capacity for sensing another's physicality in your own body

PITY—feeling sorry for someone, which can apply to ourselves as well; one of the empathy impostors

POST-TRAUMATIC STRESS DISORDER (PTSD)—a severe anxiety disorder that can develop after exposure to any event that results in psychological trauma

PRIMARY CELL THEORY—the theory that at a certain stage of embryonic development we develop a primary cell that embodies our full consciousness, chakras, meridians, and mind

QUANTUM ENTANGLEMENT—the phenomenon in which two particles, people, or objects, once connected, are forever linked

RADIANT EMPATHY—the energetic transmission of empathy

SHAMANIC EMPATHY—the empathic style that includes all other styles as well as the ability to contact other dimensions and time periods

SOUL FRAGMENTATION—the theory that illnesses, including emotional and mental ones, can be caused by a split or fragmentation of the soul

SPIRIT-TO-SPIRIT—one of the three tools for safely developing empathic gifts (see chapter 5)

SPIRITUAL EMPATHY—sensing the heart of the Divine and having the ability to determine what the Divine wants or does not want for self or other; intuitively feeling another person's level of honesty or dishonesty

SPIRITUAL GIFTS—innate psychic abilities, the terms for which begin with *clair*: clairvoyance, claircognizance, etc.

SUBTLE ENERGY—energy is information that moves; subtle energy is information in motion that cannot be perceived with the five physical senses

SYMPATHY/ENMESHMENT—entering another's subjective reality and becoming so entangled that it's hard to tell where you end and someone or something else begins; one of the empathy impostors

WOUNDED SELF—the part of us that carries the energetic impressions of past pain, anger, or shame

Resource Recommendations

Following are recommendations for learning more about empathy.

Books

Ted Andrews, *Animal-Speak: The Spiritual & Magical Powers of Creatures Great & Small*. St. Paul, MN: Llewellyn Publications, 2004.

Elaine Aron, *The Highly Sensitive Person: How to Thrive When the World Overwhelms You*. New York: Broadway, 1996.

Echo Bodine, *The Gift: Understand and Develop Your Psychic Abilities*. Novato, CA: New World Library, 2003.

Pema Chödrön, *Start Where You Are: A Guide to Compassionate Living*. Boston: Shambhala, 2004.

Catherine Crawford, *The Highly Intuitive Child: A Guide to Understanding and Parenting Unusually Sensitive and Empathic Children*. Berkeley, CA: Hunter House, 2009.

The Dalai Lama, *The Dalai Lama's Little Book of Inner Peace: The Essential Life and Teachings*. Charlottesville, VA: Hampton Roads, 2009.

Cyndi Dale, *Energetic Boundaries*. Boulder, CO: Sounds True, 2011.

———, *The Everyday Clairvoyant: Extraordinary Answers to Finding Love, Destiny, and Balance In Your Life.* Woodbury, MN: Llewellyn, 2010.

———, *The Intuition Guidebook: How to Safely and Wisely Use Your Sixth Sense.* Minneapolis, MN: Deeper Well, 2011.

Frans De Wall, *The Age of Empathy: Nature's Lessons for a Kinder Society.* New York: Crown, 2010.

John Edward, *Infinite Quest: Develop Your Psychic Intuition to Take Charge of Your Life.* New York: Sterling Ethos: 2012.

Daniel Goleman, *Emotional Intelligence.* New York: Bantam, 2006.

———, *Social Intelligence: The New Science of Human Relationships.* New York: Bantam, 2006.

Michael Harner, *The Way of the Shaman.* San Francisco: HarperSanFrancisco, 1990.

William W. A. Hewitt, *Psychic Development for Beginners: An Easy Guide to Releasing and Developing Your Psychic Abilities.* St. Paul, MN: Llewellyn, 1996.

Sandra Ingerman, *Shamanic Journeying: A Beginner's Guide.* Boulder, CO: Sounds True, 2008.

Penny Peirce, *The Intuitive Way.* Hillsboro, OR: Beyond Words, 1997.

Maia Szalavitz and Bruce D. Perry, MD, PhD, *Born for Love: Why Empathy is Essential—and Endangered.* New York: HarperCollins, 2010.

Carl Weschcke and Joe H. Slate, *The Llewellyn Complete Book of Psychic Empowerment: A Compendium of Tools and Techniques for Growth and Transformation.* Woodbury, MN: Llewellyn, 2011.

Ted Zeff, PhD, *The Highly Sensitive Person's Survival Guide: Essential Skills for Living Well in an Overstimulating World.* Oakland, CA: New Harbinger, 2004.

CDs—Audio

Cyndi Dale, *Energy Clearing*. Boulder: CO, Sounds True, 2009.

Sandra Ingerman, *The Beginner's Guide to Shamanic Journeying*. Boulder, CO: Sounds True, 2003.

Judith Orloff, MD, *Emotional Freedom Practices*. Boulder, CO: Sounds True, 2009.

DVDs

Stephen R. Covey, *Empathic Listening,* Amazon Digital Services, 2010. Kindle version with audio/visual.

Cyndi Dale, *Essential Energy Healing Techniques*. Minneapolis, MN: Deeper Well Publishing, 2013.

Judith Orloff, MD, *Emotional Freedom Now!* Boulder, CO: Gaiam, 2009.

Notes

1   Carol Kinsey Goman, "The Body Language of Empathy,"
    www.leehopkins.com/ckg-body-language-of-empathy.html.

2   Ibid.

3   Daniel Goleman, "Mirror Neurons," http://blog.gaiam.com/quotes
    /topics/mirror-neurons.

4   Society for Neuroscience, "Mirror, Mirror in the Brain: Mirror Neurons,
    Self-Understanding, and Autism Research," http://tinyurl.com/qcv5yc.

5   A. Lutz, J. Brefczynski-Lewis, and T. Johnstone, et al., "Regulation of
    the Neural Circuitry of Emotion by Compassion Meditation: Effects of
    Meditative Expertise." *PLOS One.* 2008; 3(3):e1897.

6   Mariana Lozada, Paola D'Adamo, and Miguel Angel Fuentes, "Rewarding
    Altruism," http://www.santafe.edu/media/workingpapers/10-07-014.pdf.

7   Arien Van der Merwe, "Neuropeptides: The Molecules of Emotions,"
    www.healthstresswellness.com/index.asp?pgid=72.

8   N. J. Cicutti, C. E. Smyth, O. P. Rosaeg, and M. Wilkinson, "Oxytocin
    Receptor Binding in Rat and Human Heart," BioInfoBank Library,
    http://lib.bioinfo.pl/paper:10579742.

9   Lozada, et al., "Rewarding Altruism," 2–5.

10 J. A. Bartz and E. Hollander, "Oxytocin and Experimental Therapeutics in Autism Spectrum Disorders," *Progress in Brain Research* 170 (2008): 451–62.

S. Jacob, C. W. Brune, C. S. Carter, B. L. Leventhal, C. Lord, and E. H. Cook, "Association of the Oxytocin Receptor Gene (OXTR) in Caucasian Children and Adolescents with Autism," *Neuroscience Letters* 417, 1 (April 2007): 6–9.

A. J. Guastella, E. L. Einfeld, K. Gray, N. Rinehart, B. Tonge, T. J. Lambert, and I. B. Hickie, "Intranasal Oxytocin Improves Emotion Recognition for Youth with Autism Spectrum Disorders," *Biological Psychiatry* 67, 7 (April 2010): 692–4.

11 Lozada, et al., "Rewarding Altruism," 2–5.

12 Ibid., 1–5.

13 Ibid., 5.

14 HeartMath, "The Heart Has Its Own 'Brain' and Consciousness," http://in5d.com/heart-has-brain-and-consciousness.html.

15 Rollin McCraty, "The Energetic Heart: Bioelectromagnetic Communication Within and Between People." Chapter published in *Clinical Applications of Bioelectromagnetic Medicine* (New York: Marcel Dekker, 2004), 541–62.

16 Clara Moskowitz, "Weird! Quantum Engtanglement Can Reach into the Past," www.livescience.com/19975-spooky-quantum-entanglement.html.

17 NES Health, "Finding a Framework for Energetic Medicine," http://tinyurl.com/om9klqg.

R. W. Hunt, et al., "Electromagnetic Biostimulation of Living Cultures for Biotechnology, Biofuel and Bioenergy Applications," *International Journal of Molecular Sciences*, http://tinyurl.com/n7ag4mo.

The Vatic Project, "The Kaznacheyev Experiments—ELM's Cause Disease in Cells?" http://tinyurl.com/lkty8qy.

18 Ken Costello, "Nature of Light and a Modern View of the Atom," http://tinyurl.com/kn8gqjq.

19 Mind Matters, ed. "Do Animals Feel Empathy?" http://tinyurl.com/mm8zypa.

20 Virginia Gewin, "Rats Free Each Other From Cages," *Nature: International Weekly Journal of Science*, http://tinyurl.com/d7fwhj9.

21 Mind Matters, ed. "Do Animals Feel Empathy?"

22 "The Secret Life of Plants," www.pureinsight.org/node/1496.

23 A. P. Dubrove and V. N. Pushkin, *Parapsychology and Contemporary Science* (New York: Consultants Bureau, 1982), 93–97.

24 Ross Heaven, "Plant Spirit Shamanism: Plant Communication," http://tinyurl.com/nswucpk.

25 Dubrove and Pushkin, *Parapsychology and Contemporary Science*, 93–97.

26 Don Kennedy, "Interactive Plants React and Convey Emotions," www.diginfo.tv/v/12-0050-r-en.php.

27 "Buddhist Tales for Young & Old: Volume 1," http://www .buddhanet.net/e-learning/buddhism/bt1_37.htm.

28 Miller McPherson, Lynn Smith-Lovin, and Matthew E. Brashears, "Social Isolation in America: Changes in Core Discussion Networks over Two Decades," *Journal Storage*, http://tinyurl.com/nphsd9n.

29 Ed Diener and Martin E. P. Seligman, "Beyond Money: Toward an Economy of Well-Being," www.ppc.sas.upenn.edu/articlediener.pdf.

J. S. House, K. R. Landis, and D. Umberson, "Social Relationships and Health," http://tinyurl.com/lw4g9j5.

James R. Doty, "The Science of Compassion," The Center for Compassion and Altruism Research and Education, http://tinyurl.com/md9ma4q.

30 Douglas LaBier, "America's Continuing Empathy Deficit Disorder," http://tinyurl.com/p6zk35t.

31 James R. Doty, "The Science of Compassion," http://tinyurl.com/md9ma4q.

32 Babylonian Talmud, tractate Shabbat 31a, halakhah.com/pdf/moed /Shabbath.pdf.

33 Asghar Ali Engineer, "The Concept of Compassion in Islam," http://tinyurl.com/n35pfdm.

34 Buddha Vacana: Sacred Literature of Buddhism, http://tinyurl.com/kb567yo.

35 Bhikkhu Bodhi, *The Noble Eightfold Path: Way to the End of Suffering.* (Buddhist Publication Society, 1994), 39.

36 John D. Mayer, "What Emotional Intelligence Is and Is Not," http://tinyurl.com/o7dkllw.

37 Ibid.

Peter Salovey and John D. Mayer, "Emotional Intelligence," http://tinyurl.com/msbdwxx.

38 John D. Mayer, Peter Salovey, and David R. Caruso, "What Does Emotional Intelligence Predict?" University of New Hampshire, http://tinyurl.com/pekq33f.

39 S. Hein, "The Dark Side of Emotional Intelligence," http://eqi.org/dark1.htm.

40 Daniel Goleman, "Primal Leadership: Learning to Lead with Emotional Intelligence," Center for Building a Culture of Empathy, http://tinyurl.com/qjberre.

41 "Call to the Wild: 7 Amazing Animal Whisperers," http://tinyurl.com/o9s2sno.

42 John Muir, www.goodreads.com/author/quotes/5297.

43 Michael Cobley, *Seeds of Earth* (New York: Hachette, 2009), 50.

44 President Barack Obama, www.brainyquote.com/quotes/keywords /grace.html.

45 Janice M. Morse, Carl Mitcham, and Wim J. van Der Steen, "Compathy or Physical Empathy: Implications for the Caregiver Relationship." *Journal of Medical Humanities*, vol. 19, no. 1 (1998), 51065, DOI: 10.1023A:1024988002129.

46 Vesica Institute for Holistic Studies, www.vesica.org.

47 National Alliance on Mental Illness, *The Iris*, vol. 27, issue 5, September/October 2012, http://tinyurl.com/mk3n5yx.

48 "Mental Disorders," Armenian Medical Network, www.health.am/psy/disorders.

49 Liansheng Lui, et al., "Transient Gastric Irritation in the Neonatal Rats Leads to Changes in Hypothalamic CRF Expression, Depression- and Anxiety-Like Behavior as Adults," http://tinyurl.com/mw8vzsv.

50 Jim and Amy Hallowes, "Being Highly Sensitive," http://tinyurl.com/lyonjku.

51 "Effects of Stress on Brain Development," Better Brains for Babies, http://tinyurl.com/kvs7bkl.

52 American Psychiatric Association, *Diagnostic and Statistical Manual of Mental Disorders: DSM-IV* (Washington, DC: American Psychiatric Association, 1994).

53 R. Yehuda, S. L. Halligan, J. A. Golier, R. Grossman, and L. M. Bierer, "Effects of Trauma Exposure on the Cortisol Response to Dexamethasone Administration in PTSD and Major Depressive Disorder," *Psychoneuroendocrinology* 29, 3 (2004): 389–404.

R. Yehuda, S. L. Halligan, R. Grossman, J. A. Golier, and C. Wong, "The Cortisol and Glucocorticoid Receptor Response to Low Dose Dexamethasone Administration in Aging Combat Veterans and Holocaust Survivors with and without Posttraumatic Stress Disorder," *Biol Psychiatry* 52, 5 (2002): 393–403.

54 D. Ingleby, ed. *Critical Psychiatry: The Politics of Mental Health* (London: Free Association, 2004.)

55 "What Is Depression?" National Institute of Mental Health, http://tinyurl.com/cqpgx29.

56 Lynn E. O'Connor, et al., "Empathy and Depression: The Moral System on Overdrive," Emotions, Personality & Altruism Research Group, www.eparg.org/publications/empathy-chapter-web.pdf, 49–55.

57 Simone Shamay-Tsoory, et al., "Neuropsychological Evidence of Impaired Cognitive Empathy in Euthymic Bipolar Disorder," *The American Journal of Psychiatry*, http://tinyurl.com/lb5prop.

58 Roxanne Dryden-Edwards, "Biopolar Disorder (Mania)," www.medicinenet.com/bipolar_disorder/article.htm.

59 Ibid., 60.

60 Simone Shamay-Tsoory, et al., "Neuropsychological Evidence of Impaired Cognitive Empathy in Euthymic Bipolar Disorder."

61 John M. Grohol, "Borderline Personality Disorder," http://tinyurl.com/qxt2k5o.

62 Eric A. Fertuck, "Borderline 'Empathy' Revisited," http://tinyurl.com/mmdbney.

63 Haven, "How the Brain Sees Empathy in Borderline Personality Disorder—Part I," *Beyond the Borderline Personality*, http://tinyurl.com/lqw7myt.

64 Robert A. Emmons, "Narcissism: Theory and Measurement,"
    www.sakkyndig.com/psykologi/artvit/emmons1987.pdf.

    Randi Kreger, "Lack of Empathy: The Most Telling Narcissistic Trait,"
    http://tinyurl.com/7ykkw5v.

65 K. Ritter, I. Dziobek, et al., "Lack of Empathy in Patients with Narcissistic
    Personality Disorder," www.ncbi.nlm.nih.gov/pubmed/21055831.

66 Hugo Schwyzer, "Empathy Can Be Learned: Overcoming Narcissism,
    One Day at a Time," http://tinyurl.com/lxfasjd.

67 Kevin Dutton, "The Wisdom of Psychopaths," *Scientific American,*
    vol. 307, no. 4 (October 2012): 76–79.

68 Lynn E. O'Connor, et al., "Empathy and Depression: The Moral System
    on Overdrive," Emotions, Personality & Altruism Research Group,
    www.eparg.org/publications/empathy-chapter-web.pdf.

69 A. A. Marsh and E. M. Cardinale, "When Psychopathy Impairs Moral
    Judgments: Neural Responses During Judgments About Causing Fear,"
    Soc Cogn Affect Neurosci (2012 Sep 5) [Epub ahead of print] PubMed
    PMID: 22956667.

70 "Bullies May Enjoy Seeing Others in Pain: Brain Scans Show Disruption
    in Natural Empathic Response," *UChicagoNews,* 2008,
    http://tinyurl.com/oav3t27.

71 "Psychopathy and Empathy," www.partiallyexaminedlife
    .com/2012/07/20/psychopathy-and-empathy.

72 David Sack, "What Makes Addicts Stop Caring? How Empathy Gets
    Hijacked by Addiction," http://tinyurl.com/lj6nbj7.

73 J. Lee, J. Zaki, et al., "Schizophrenia Patients Are Impaired
    in Empathic Accuracy," William James Hall, Harvard Edu.,
    http://tinyurl.com/m6gudd6.

74 Sharon Perkins, "The Negative Symptoms of Schizophrenia,"
    http://tinyurl.com/curxhjk.

75 Maureen Roberts, "Schizophrenia…Soul In Crisis,"
    www.psychiatrywithsoul.com/Schizophrenia.html.

76 Melinda Wenner, "Infected with Insanity: Could Microbes
    Cause Mental Illness?" http://tinyurl.com/ln9zxob.

    "Mental Health Treatment That Works," http://tinyurl.com/ozej4xr.

77 "Psychotic Disorders," http://tinyurl.com/d4jym8.

78 "What Is Austism?" www.autismspeaks.org/what-autism.

79 G. J. Taylor, R. M. Bagby, et al., *Disorders of Affect Regulation: Alexithymia in Medical and Psychiatric Illness* (Cambridge University Press, 1997).

80 Phoebe Caldwell, "Can We Talk? Autism for Us," http://tinyurl.com/oamrb2a.

81 R. Burnier, G. Dawson, S. Webb, and M. Murias, "EEG Mu Rhythm and Imitation Impairments in Individuals with Autism Spectrum Disorder," http://tinyurl.com/o75wwrb.

82 Randall D. Ladnier, *Treating ADHD as Attachment Deficit Hyperactivity Disorder*, http://tinyurl.com/q99aq4m, 32–34.

83 Ibid., 35.

84 "The Hasmonean Dynasty from (John) Hyrcanus to (Salome) Alexandra (134-67 BCE)," www.abu.nb.ca/courses/ntintro/intest/hist4.htm.

85 "Epigenetics & Applications," http://tinyurl.com/om5n6xq.

"Ghost in Your Genes," *Nova*. www.pbs.org/wgbh/nova/transcripts/3413_genes.html.

"Epigentics: When the Environment Modifies the Genes." Douglas Mental Health Institute University, www.douglas.qc.ca/info/epigenetics.

David Crews, et al., "Epigenetic Transgenerational Inheritance of Altered Stress Responses," Proceedings of the National Academy of Sciences, http://tinyurl.com/mu5eef6.

86 Grant McFetridge, "The Primary Cell: Understanding the Subcellular Basis of Consciousness, Spiritual Experiences, Trauma and Disease," Institute for the Study of Peak States, http://tinyurl.com/lhbfp5c.

87 Sandra L. Brown, "Genetic and Neuro-Physiologic Basis for Hyper-Empathy," http://tinyurl.com/nlbj6us.

88 Lynn E. O'Connor, et al., "Empathy and Depression: The Moral System on Overdrive," Emotions, Personality & Altruism Research Group, www.eparg.org/publications/empathy-chapter-web.pdf, 51–62.

GET MORE AT LLEWELLYN.COM

Visit us online to browse hundreds of our books and decks, plus sign up to receive our e-newsletters and exclusive online offers.

- **Free tarot readings** • **Spell-a-Day** • **Moon phases**
- **Recipes, spells, and tips** • **Blogs** • **Encyclopedia**
- **Author interviews, articles, and upcoming events**

GET SOCIAL WITH LLEWELLYN

Find us on Facebook

www.Facebook.com/LlewellynBooks

Follow us on twitter™

www.Twitter.com/Llewellynbooks

GET BOOKS AT LLEWELLYN

LLEWELLYN ORDERING INFORMATION

 Order online: Visit our website at www.llewellyn.com to select your books and place an order on our secure server.

 Order by phone:
- Call toll free within the U.S. at 1-877-NEW-WRLD (1-877-639-9753)
- Call toll free within Canada at 1-866-NEW-WRLD (1-866-639-9753)
- We accept VISA, MasterCard, and American Express

 Order by mail:
Send the full price of your order (MN residents add 6.875% sales tax) in U.S. funds, plus postage and handling to: Llewellyn Worldwide, 2143 Wooddale Drive Woodbury, MN 55125-2989

POSTAGE AND HANDLING

STANDARD (U.S. & Canada):
(Please allow 12 business days)
$25.00 and under, add $4.00.
$25.01 and over, FREE SHIPPING.

INTERNATIONAL ORDERS (airmail only):
$16.00 for one book, plus $3.00 for each additional book.

Visit us online for more shipping options. Prices subject to change.

FREE CATALOG!

To order, call
1-877-
NEW-WRLD
ext. 8236
or visit our
website